Clayton Kershaw

Biography

Journey To The
Greatness In
Baseball History

TABLE OF CONTENTS

CHAPTER 1
UNYIELDING CYCLE

*T*he five-day cycle would soon resume, so Clayton Kershaw attempted to describe how it had defined his existence over the previous twenty years. He pressed his fingers into the kitchen table. The benefits of the cycle surrounded him. The fireplace crackled in the main room. Above it hung a row of stockings, one for each of his four children. A pile of Amazon Prime shipments sat near the front entrance. That night, Santa Claus will travel on the back of a fire truck to greet the families of Highland Park, the affluent Dallas suburb where Kershaw had spent the majority of his life. Christmas was two weeks away.

When Kershaw invited me to his house in the winter of 2022, he had only been at a crossroads for two months. He had been in this situation before, and he would go through it again. He had decided to continue playing, which entailed dividing his life into five-day periods. This was the norm for pitchers in Major League Baseball. They spend four days preparing. On the fifth day, they perform. This cycle formed Kershaw, enriching him while also tormenting him.

For more than fifteen years, the fate of the Los Angeles Dodgers—one of baseball's glitziest, most prestigious franchises, a financial behemoth worth approximately $4 billion, winners of eleven division titles, three National League pennants, and the 2020 World Series—has revolved around Clayton Kershaw's fifth day. He was the best left-handed pitcher of his generation, a spiritual successor to Sandy Koufax. On his journey to becoming a ten-time All-Star, three-time Cy Young Award winner, and the first pitcher to win the National League MVP award since Bob Gibson, Kershaw relished the four days of training, the camaraderie of teammates, and the trappings of athletic success. As he approached his thirty-fifth birthday, he wondered if he could continue in this pattern indefinitely. But then he remembered how he felt on the previous pitching day.

"It's only the fifth day, and it's a lot," Kershaw remarked. "The stress." The preparation. The pain. All of that stuff takes its toll."

For once, his body didn't hurt. During the summer of 2022, he suffered from severe back pain. The majority of pitches were uncomfortable. Most mornings, he awoke with apprehension: Will my back pain today? The soreness subsided after some rest and therapy. He felt better than in the previous winter. After an elbow issue forced him to miss the 2021 postseason, Kershaw was concerned that he would require his first surgery. He avoided surgery, but he was constantly reminded of his newfound weakness. He couldn't wash his hair or write his name. When he took up a baseball to toss again, his elbow complained for a month. "But I kept throwing," he explained. "And finally it got better."

As a result, he repeated what he had done every spring since his childhood. He went to spring training with the Dodgers. He had turned down the option to sign with his local Texas Rangers, his childhood favorite team, which is run by his Highland Park neighbor, longtime friend, and old training partner Chris Young. When Kershaw informed Young that he was returning to Los Angeles, "It broke my heart," Young said. Young wondered if he'd get another chance. The idea of Kershaw leaving the Dodgers seemed ridiculous.

Kershaw's Dodger Stadium debut came two months after his twentieth birthday. He soon established the industry norm. He starred as few others had before him. He had to bear the consequences of his accomplishments. "He's gotten some injuries over the years, where you're always like, 'This might be the one,'" former teammate Zack Greinke said. "And then it seems to never be the end of it." Kershaw had just damaged his hip cartilage, ripped a lat muscle, frayed tendons near his elbow, and herniated a disk in his back. He'd recovered from each of them without surgery, but the toll was growing. Some of his maladies were the inevitable result of a job centered on the unnatural act of constantly throwing a sphere overhand. Some of it stemmed from his unusual delivery, the massive thud of his six-foot-four, 225-pound frame striking the ground, and the vicious trajectory of his left arm behind it. "It's like a car crash every time he throws," remarked another former teammate. Some of it was due to Kershaw's rare blend of precociousness and effectiveness. He was so good, so young, and relied on so much that there had to be a cost.

By the end of 2015, when he was twenty-seven and had already won three Cy Young awards, he had accumulated more than 1,600 innings, a figure topped by only two other pitchers at that age during the previous thirty-five years. CC Sabathia never made an All-Star squad after the age of 32. After the age of thirty-three, Félix Hernández never pitched again in the majors. Kershaw started the All-Star Game at Dodger Stadium in 2022, when he was 34 years old. The distinction acted as a farewell as Kershaw approached the sunset, but it was not without merit. He finished the season with a 2.28 earned-run average, outperforming all but five other pitchers. Even in his decline, few could touch him. His career earned-run average of 2.48 was the lowest among starting pitchers since 1920, surpassing Koufax, Pedro Martínez, Greg Maddux, and all others.

The 2022 season concluded earlier than predicted. The 111-win Dodgers had lost to the upstart San Diego Padres. Kershaw lost his only postseason start. A few years ago, his performance would have resulted in cries about his incapacity to compete in the playoffs. However, Kershaw softened that narrative when he won two games for the winning Dodgers in the 2020 World Series. The triumph capped a seven-year crucible of October pain and marked the final box on his Baseball Hall of Fame resume. Others wondered about the end as the injuries piled up, his children grew older, and the stress of the five-day cycle increased. "At this point," replied A. J. Ellis, Kershaw's former catcher and one of his closest friends, says, "It's like, what keeps him going?"

Two months before another spring training, Kershaw was thinking less about why he kept going and more about why he may quit. His children. His back, shoulders, or hips. He stated that he might resign for a more fundamental cause. The load of greatness, the standard he had set for himself, the strain of being Clayton Kershaw—all of it was becoming increasingly difficult to bear. He could only give his all so often.

"That's ultimately what will drive you to stop, when it becomes too much to get ready for that day, every day," according to Kershaw. "I probably put more stress on it than most."

One July day in 2013, a movie star paid a visit to the Dodgers' clubhouse. This was not unusual for Hollywood's home squad, except for two details: the star arrived late. And the star arrived on a day when Clayton Kershaw was pitching.

When the man entered the room, the crowd surged. The athletes shouted catchphrases that have been immortalized on film. As the Dodgers yelled about motherfucking snakes on motherfucking planes, Kershaw stewed at his locker, dressed in full uniform with his No. 22 across his back. He put on a jacket, which he wore before every start, with "that zipper that zips all the way to the top no matter if it's April or July in fucking Miami," one former colleague remarked.

Kershaw stood up. He clutched a baseball in his left hand, as he normally did. His right hand held his black Wilson 2000A CK22 glove, which he has worn since his rookie season. He was both a product and a captive of routine. He assumed his adherence to habit would carry him through the 162-game season. Others said it made him prone to failure in high-pressure situations. In his early years, before the game humbled him and launched him on a quest for answers, he would stick to his meticulously planned routine. The plan was for him to come into the Dodgers dugout at 6:20 p.m. He didn't have a moment to spare, even for Hollywood royalty.

"Clayton!" the actor exclaimed, holding up a hand as Kershaw walked by. "My man!"

Kershaw would not meet his gaze. He kept his death stare for later, when he encountered the team official who had scheduled the visit. He stormed out. He left Samuel L. Jackson hanging.

It was worse before he was a father.

Cali Ann Kershaw's father had developed a reputation for beating opponents during games and scaring teammates before her birth in January 2015. Kershaw worked hard and was a pleasant presence throughout the four days between starts. On sunny days, he wore outmoded flip-down sunglasses in the dugout. On the team plane, he played cards and let off some righteous flatulence. While strolling through the cafeteria one afternoon, he snatched a chicken finger from a teammate's child's plate. He portrayed healthy goofiness. "He's the only guy I ever played with," remarked former teammate Dan Haren, "who I would let date my wife."

The fifth day was different.

It began before he got to the ballpark. "You wake up in a mood where you don't want to talk," Kershaw explained. He was silent but not motionless, his legs twitching, his mind racing, and his heart pounding. He considered vomiting. He wasn't exactly angry or nervous, despite appearances. He just felt overwhelmed by the task at hand, which was to climb atop the pitcher's mound alone and be Clayton Kershaw. He despised interactions, even with Ellen. "I don't want to waste my breath," Kershaw added. "I couldn't even get the words out."

Skip Johnson, a local pitching expert, tutored Kershaw prior to his last high school season. Johnson scarcely charged Kershaw for his lessons. Kershaw never forgot the compassion. Years later, the University of Oklahoma hired Johnson as its baseball coach. When Johnson received the job, he texted Kershaw. It took two messages for Kershaw to answer. Kershaw, who had been concerned about an emergency, sounded ecstatic when Johnson broke the news. Johnson begged for a favor. The athletic department was preparing a press release. Could Kershaw say anything nice about him? "Skip, I can't give you a quote," Kershaw replied. "I'm pitching tonight."

After Ellen moved to Los Angeles after their wedding in December 2010, the couple watched television to get through those fifth days. Clayton watched CSI episodes prior to the show's launch. Ellen learnt not to annoy him. The edict was distributed inside his inner circle. He rarely returned calls. He ignored texts. On the fifth day, his friends communicated separately over group chats. Kershaw hid his morning misanthropy after the birth of Cali, who was followed by boys Charley, Cooper and Chance. Instead of watching Grissom and Willows solve cases, he spent his time with "the kiddos," as he called them. The kids used him like a bearded jungle gym. "He, at all times, has one of the kids in his lap, wrestling him, hugging him," Ellen told me.

When Kershaw became a parent, the metamorphosis occurred as he drove to work. When he arrived, he changed into his outfit, spikes and all. "That's not normal," former teammate Tony Watson stated. Several hours before a game of A. J. Ellis' minor league managers paid a visit to the clubhouse. The man made a request. "My son," the manager explained, "is a huge Clayton Kershaw fan. Is there any chance he can autograph a baseball for him?" Ellis realized the concept was risky. But he decided it was worth the risk. Kershaw did not say anything. He scribbled his name and stared at Ellis the entire time.

Kershaw saved syllables but created noise. He paced the clubhouse, bouncing baseballs against the walls. He flipped curveballs, burning off energy and looking for the correct feel. In his early years, veterans such as catcher Brad Ausmus attempted to grab the ball and loosen Kershaw up. It never worked. Kershaw's pranks came to an end as his reputation increased. "You felt like the season was on the line every time he pitched," ex-teammate Skip Schumaker remarked. The atmosphere fluctuated between edgy and celebratory. Tension blended with the excitement of working with the world's top pitcher. Former Dodger reliever J. P. Howell dubbed Kershaw "Off Day" because no one else was required when he began. Another reliever declined to wear cleats in the bullpen when Kershaw threw. But nearly no one dared to goof off around him. Players are taught to look around corners and keep their ears open. If they heard "pock-pock-pock," they turned around. If they crossed his way, they averted their gaze. Some colleagues made jokes about not wanting to steal his oxygen. Everyone knew to whom the valuable resource belonged. "When he walked in, his demeanor, his attitude—it was like, 'Shit, I can't mess around today,'" former Dodgers closer Kenley Jansen explained.

Kershaw's schedule was hard-wired and did not allow any interruptions. He ate a turkey sandwich before each start, a habit he had since high school. In the majors, he made his own at the ballpark: mustard and cheese were required, lettuce and onions preferred, and mayonnaise was strictly barred. When he sat down in the clubhouse café, the chairs cleared and the conversation cooled. "You have to sit there, and you're like, 'You just sucked all the energy out of the room because of your psychosis over having to pitch in a couple hours,'" Ellis told me.

After eating, Kershaw went to the workout room. An empty table awaited him. On his first day as a Dodger, Chase Utley jumped upon the table. Utley commanded respect throughout the sport. Even so, Dodgers massage therapist Yosuke Nakajima advised him to move. "He'll be here in about three minutes," Nakajima explained. "I suggest you get up." Nakajima, who had worked as a massage therapist with the Dodgers for over two decades and was affectionately referred to as "Possum," was Kershaw's gatekeeper. Jansen frequently lounged on the table before Kershaw arrived. "That is Kershaw's table!"Nakajima would say. "Get up!"The personnel prepared the space for him. Kershaw needed a Red Bull and a protein bar. Late in his stay in Los Angeles, third baseman Justin Turner barged into the room, starving from a workout. He ate the protein bar that was sitting on the table. Nakajima screamed out, "What are you doing?Turner asked Nakajima to find a replacement.

The training room was Kershaw's sacred domain. When he came, fully dressed, cleats on but unlaced, he dominated the real estate. There was always a baseball game on TV. He demanded silence. Kershaw once threatened utility player Kiké Hernández for broadcasting a Snapchat video.

Few guys are so great that their limitations define them. Clayton Kershaw was one of them for quite some time.

Kershaw's dominance established an image of invincibility. "To be that good every year, for that long, it's fucking impossible," former teammate Alex Wood remarked. Friend and foe both used the same words to characterize him. "To me, he's the greatest left-handed pitcher of all time," New York Yankees starter Gerrit Cole said. Madison Bumgarner, a longstanding rival of San Francisco, was less ambiguous. "I think he's the best pitcher to ever play," Bumgarner added. Brandon Belt, another former Giant, described Kershaw as "the best pitcher that I faced, every single year in the big leagues." Greinke had been in the majors for twenty seasons. "I think the best of any pitcher I've played with," he remarked. Paul Goldschmidt, a longtime National League West rival, described Kershaw as "my favorite guy in baseball." My favorite player. "I hate to say that about a pitcher."

Although Kershaw threw hard, others threw harder. His curveball and slider were crisp, but his other pitches were nastier. He was a large man with an unusual delivery, but others were taller and moved in bizarre ways. "You have to look at the man, how competitive he is," former Giants manager Bruce Bochy stated. "It doesn't work unless you have that inside you." To Andrew Friedman, the architect of the Dodgers' late-aughts powerhouse, Kershaw was "the greatest competitor I've ever seen firsthand." Brandon McCarthy, a teammate for several seasons, questioned if Kershaw's ability strayed into the otherworldly. "Is this only a gift?" McCarthy stated.

Which made what happened to Kershaw in October so perplexing. From 2013 to 2019, the Dodgers appeared in the postseason each year. In each of those seasons, the Dodgers failed to win the championship. Kershaw has cost his club the last game five times. Kershaw's postseason struggles grew from an unusual occurrence to a national obsession. He became the central character of October baseball. Why couldn't he accomplish it? Why couldn't he win everything? When would he lift the World Series title, which had eluded his team for so long? The Dodgers hadn't referred to themselves as champions since 1988, when they won the title behind the strong back of Orel Hershiser and the shaky legs of Kirk Gibson. Kershaw was meant to stop the drought. Instead, he was criticized for having extended it.

Kershaw slumped in the 2017 World Series against the Houston Astros, not realizing his opponents were using an unlawful sign-stealing technique. "I still have PTSD about that," he added. In 2019, he allowed two game-changing home runs against the Washington Nationals. In the dugout, he hung his head and glanced out at Chavez Ravine. His comrades burst into tears and simmered with hatred on his behalf. They knew how many innings he'd pitched in his twenties until his body gave out. They watched him give up a day of his valuable schedule to pitch on short rest in October, making him an outlier among his colleagues in the 2010s. "Some pitchers flat-out refuse the ball, unless they're at full strength," claimed former teammate Michael Young. "Kersh has never done that." They saw all the hours he put into his trade. They made it through his fifth day and realized how much it meant. "Every time he failed, I know how deeply that hurt him," said former teammate Josh Lindblom.

At times, teammates and friends expressed concern about Kershaw's workload. The Dodgers had bet a lot on him. He was a first-round choice, a number-one starter, and the franchise's face. From his first days as a Dodger, he was compared to Koufax, the southpaw who helped the team move from Brooklyn's Boys of Summer to the monarchs of Southern California. Former Dodger Justin Turner said, "He's the savior for the Dodgers, and he's the next Sandy Koufax for the Dodgers. That pressure on his back in following Sandy's footsteps is a real thing."

Despite a 52-year age difference, Kershaw and Koufax were buddies. But Kershaw rejected the idea that he had to follow in anyone else's shoes. "I was like, 'The next Sandy Koufax?'"I have no interest in being Sandy Koufax," Kershaw stated. "And I do not want to live up to that. I wasn't interested in being that. I had different motives and motivations.

Kershaw was responsible for the weight he carried. After the loss to the Nationals, he stood stunned inside his clubhouse. He pondered aloud if everything about his reputation as a choker was true. He peered into the abyss, only seeing himself. He realized he needed to change. So he did, in subtle and profound ways, adopting new ideas while maintaining his sense of self. When the club ultimately won the World Series a year later, after a season upended and cut short by the Covid-19 outbreak, his overarching emotion was relief. "You don't know the burden that you carry," he told you. "Because at some point, you just get used to the weight on your shoulders."

After an injury-plagued 2021 and a dismal conclusion to 2022, Kershaw reflected on the depth of his reasons and motivations. As he prepared to resume the five-day cycle, he needed to take stock. He didn't need the money. His case for Cooperstown was completed. "I have no individual goals," he stated. His body may use a break after two decades of pitching-related pain. However, the prospect of winning another championship remained appealing. The cycle loomed.

The day after Santa Claus came to Highland Park, Kershaw stood inside the kitchenette of his charity's headquarters, which is only a three-minute drive from home. He had completed a throwing session after dressing and feeding his children. He frequently told pals that his ideal career after baseball would be crossing guard at their primary school. However, he knew there would be more hours to occupy. Perhaps the family would purchase an RV and take a tour of America that was not designed around ballparks. He had traveled extensively over his job yet seen so little. He had never gone to Hawaii or continental Europe. He couldn't imagine planning a trip without time to toss. During his honeymoon at a resort in Mexico, he brought baseballs to throw into bedding pillows.

"Does part of you," I declared, "look forward to—"

"Yes," Kershaw answered. "One hundred percent."

"Like, not being in this cycle," I added.

"It'll be great," Kershaw added. I can't wait for that. Both have numerous positive aspects. "The hardest part is not wanting the other thing."

He recalled something Ellen had frequently advised him: "Don't take your time for granted." He was a rare man who could still make a fortune playing a game created for boys. Among his peers, he was the rarest of the rare, one who would be remembered long after his final pitch. He wished to commemorate that generosity. He needed to give it his all. "I'm never, like, trudging through another season," Kershaw added. "This was our decision. I did not have to play. We determined that we wanted to do it. "I wanted to do it."

RV travels, a job as a crossing guard, and decades of independence could wait. He had already consented to another year of fifth days. As a result, he believed he owed his franchise, teammates, and himself nothing less than everything.

CHAPTER 2
DRIVEN BY A DREAM

*C*layton Kershaw drove his white GMC Denali to his high school the morning after Santa Claus passed through Highland Park. He flashed a fob at the gate of Highland Park's indoor athletic facility. He was well past the days of jumping fences to throw at Scotland Yard. The school gave him access to a facility carpeted in synthetic turf and lined like a football pitch.

The facility was vacant except for a teenager kicking field goals. Kershaw threw four times a week to prepare for the season, in addition to his routine lifting, conditioning, and physical therapy. He set up throwing sessions with local pitchers. These were not open-ended situations. A few weeks later, Shawn Tolleson asked Kershaw when they could have lunch. Kershaw was precise. He told Tolleson that his session ended at 11:42 a.m., therefore noon was OK. Kershaw arrived smelling of sweat.

Several big-leaguers have previously pitched with Kershaw. Receiving an invitation seemed like an honor and privilege. The majority of his throwing partners were now gone. Tolleson retired in 2019. Yu Darvish spent the winter between Japan and San Diego. Chris Young had been named general manager of the Texas Rangers. Only one of his contemporaries remained: Brett Anderson, a massive, quiet southpaw whose career had been linked to Kershaw's since they were kids.

Kershaw was the first to arrive. The others staggered in. Anderson murmured a hello. They watched the kicker practice. His technique was unusual. He stood behind the football and kicked it without striding. It reminded the pitchers of their industry's hub for biomechanical advancement.

"That's like the Driveline of kicking right there," Anderson explained.

Kershaw ambled over.

Can I try one?He asked.

The kid moved aside. Kershaw stood behind the ball, elevated his right foot, and took a swing. The ball hardly got off the ground. It skittered into a soccer net beneath the goalposts. Kershaw jogged back to the pitchers. "I was right there," he replied.

Kershaw relaxed his arm while the others talked. The majority of the conversation was on six-foot-seven right-hander Kyle Muller. The day before, he was dealt from the Atlanta Braves to the Oakland Athletics. Muller told the group how he missed the initial phone contact from Athletics manager Mark Kotsay. He'd been too busy hunting.

Kershaw walked away. "If there's a baseball in his hand," said Jamey Wright, a former throwing partner, "it's business." Kershaw picked up a weighted ball and knelt facing away from a wall. In one action, he hurled the ball behind his back and off the wall, catching it with the same hand. The sound echoed throughout the facility. Kershaw then stepped up and farted.

Kershaw and Anderson stood eight yards apart and began playing catch. Anderson had sat out the 2022 season, but he was planning a comeback, and his motions remained lethargic and slow. He made it look easy. Kershaw groaned and thudded. He made everything appear violent. As the two men grew apart, it was easy to see why, seventeen years ago, when they were both left-handed youths dreaming the same dream, scouts looked at them and knew which one would succeed.

In the summer of 2005, 144 young boys arrived in Joplin, Missouri, a city located in the state's southwestern region. They came from Northern and Southern California, the Pacific Northwest and Miami suburbs, the sprawl outside of New Orleans, and Manhattan's Lower East Side. They represented the best of the best in the American Amateur Baseball Congress, American Legion Baseball, and all other summer leagues around the United States. They were all there for the same reason: to compete in the eleventh annual Tournament of the Stars and represent the United States at the Pan American Championships in September.

The lads were divided into eight teams. For a week, they played doubleheaders in front of Team USA officials, college coaches, and professional scouts. At night, they stayed with host families. Some of the boys were either too arrogant or too innocent to be nervous about the performance. Kershaw was not among the boys. He took notice of all the evaluators in the stands. He understood the gravity of the chance.

He had not traveled to Joplin alone. Tolleson also made the cut. However, the teams were picked at random. Kershaw hooked up with Anderson, who was already well-known for his surgical precision and preference for silence. His word-to-strike ratio was minuscule. Anderson was born into baseball. His father, Frank, was a Division I pitching coach who worked at Texas Tech, Texas, and Oklahoma State before becoming head coach in 2004. During a rain delay at one of Frank's games, preteen Brett kept himself entertained by hurling a Nerf Vortex football until the rocket-shaped device landed above the ticket office, according to Trip Couch, who worked with Frank Anderson at Texas. "He was never a very good athlete," Couch explained. "But good Lord, he had a great arm and he could hit a gnat's ass."

Anderson's reputation preceded him to Joplin. "Brett Anderson," remembered Team USA pitching coach Jason Hisey, "had the best high school command I've ever seen." He had promised to play for

17

his father following graduation, but few expected him to ever arrive in college. "He was just so much more polished than all of us," Kershaw explained. Hank Conger, a catcher from Huntington Beach, California, had known Anderson since they were twelve. Conger read every issue of Baseball America, keeping track of his peers as the next summer's draft approached. According to the newspaper, Anderson is expected to be a top-ten pick. "To me," Conger recounted, "up until that point, he was the best left-handed pitcher, amateur pitcher, in that draft." Team USA was overjoyed when Anderson agreed to play. "At that age, if you can keep walks down, you're gold," said Ray Darwin, USA Baseball's director of operations. "And so Brett Anderson was, like, the stud."

Conger and the others have less familiarity with Kershaw. Conger noticed his name but was generally teamed with his D-Bat comrades. One night early in the trials, when the boys were still nervous, Conger settled behind the plate to catch Kershaw. Prior to the trip, Conger had gotten a preliminary scouting report on Kershaw. The velocity from the left side is decent, if unpredictable, with a large curveball. Kershaw was undervalued in the report. The fastball was lively. The curve was "an absolute hammer," Conger recalled. Conger couldn't understand why Kershaw landed in Joplin with little fanfare.

Who the fuck is this guy? Conger wondered.

Clayton Kershaw played a position that was unique to his ability and geography that summer. College coaches, professional scouts, and accredited magazines regarded him as one of the country's best high school pitchers. He was also the third starter for D-Bat. The travel-ball club had a talent who would enter the spring as Baseball America's top high school player in the country. His name was Jordan Walden.

Walden lived in Mansfield, almost an hour south of Highland Park.

Despite the fact that Walden did not participate in the Team USA tryouts, he demonstrated skills that would make major league organizations salivate. He stood six feet four and weighed 185 pounds. His right arm appeared blessed. He threw hard. When he appeared at a Texas Christian University showcase that summer, scouts measured him at 99 mph—harder than Walden thought he could throw. Walden benefited from an unusual delivery in which he jumped down the slope of the mound. The leap reduced the distance to the plate, so amplifying his heater. "Nobody could touch him," said Walden's former D-Bat and Mansfield High teammate, Mark Cohoon. However, when D-Bat coach Ken Guthrie needed to win, he chose another of his pitchers. "Tolleson," he remembered, "was the go-to guy." To Guthrie, who had played a few seasons of pro ball, Tolleson already possessed a big-league slider. Tolleson "was absolutely just unhittable," according to D-Bat catcher and future major leaguer Cameron Rupp. "Shawn was the first guy I ever saw strike seven kids out in a row," she said.

Kershaw couldn't throw as hard as Walden. His curveball couldn't equal Tolleson's slider. According to D-Bat authorities, Kershaw provided an intriguing blend of brains, aptitude, and ambition. "The biggest asset he had was how competitive he was," Guthrie said. He was eager to do anything to attain his goal. Earlier that summer, Kershaw was invited to the Area Code Games, a prominent competition for schoolboy talent in Long Beach, California. Kershaw listened to a presentation by Alan Jaeger, a former college pitcher whose unique methods had captivated major-league stars such as Barry Zito, another lefty with a powerful curveball. Kershaw followed Jaeger's warm up routines "to the letter," he recalls.

In addition to the showcases, the D-Bat guys competed in dozens of games that summer. There were weekday doubleheaders and weekend tournaments. There were usually more innings than arms. "They'd say, 'Hey, we're going to this tournament in Oklahoma City.

We need two pitchers. Can you call a friend?"recalled Austin Goolsby, a catcher from Coppell, Texas. Before a tournament in Oklahoma, Guthrie scouted the area for pitchers. One of his assistant coaches had scouted a lefty who had recently relocated from California. Guthrie called Greg Britton to see if his son, Zack, was available. Guthrie picked up Zack at a Cabela's in Fort Worth— "back when that was okay to do, I guess," Britton said—and drove his new pitcher to the tournament. Britton grew up in Weatherford, a rural community, and did not fit in with the privileged children of Dallas. One of the first players to approach him was Kershaw. "If you need anything," Kershaw said to Britton, "here's my number."

Britton moved to the back of the rotation alongside Kershaw. "Shawn Tolleson and Jordan Walden were just so much better, at that age," according to Britton. That weekend, Kershaw threw in a prelim game. Britton began the championship game. Around the third inning, Guthrie saw rustling in the dugout. "I want the ball," Kershaw muttered. Guthrie did not want his pitchers to throw more than once per week. He held off Kershaw till the last inning. Guthrie put a tight leash on Kershaw: if he threw more than twelve pitches, he was out. "And of course, he went out there and struck out everybody in less than twelve pitches," Guthrie told me.

Kershaw compiled a list of slights. Cade Griffis once said, "Someone told him he had a horseshit pickoff move." Kershaw stewed on it all offseason. He dominated the opposition in a game the following summer. His fastball averaged approximately 85 mph, which was still quicker than most amateurs could handle. Griffis was watching the sequence of outs when Kershaw hammered a hitter. Kershaw then picked off the runner at first base.

"Clayton," Griffis inquired later, "did you hit that guy on purpose?"

Kershaw gave a sheepish smile. "I just wanted to see if I could pick him off," he told me.

Some of the other D-Bat players felt Kershaw was aware of the gap between himself and his celebrated contemporaries. He realized he was pretty decent. He wanted to be great.

Baseball hinges about failure. It is intended to shatter the fan's heart, but it first breaks the participants' will. Failure affects every player. They fail due to incompetence, frailty, or temperament. The fortunate few overcome their failures. The vast majority do not. For them, the pain of the game is frequently not their failure. It's that there were so many days when failing seemed impossible.

In the summer of 2005, at the Tournament of Stars in Joplin, there were a few youngsters who appeared unaffected by failure. They were the types of players that other players muttered about. Everyone gawked while they took batting practice or threw bullpens. "They almost take on a mythical quality when you see them walking around," said Lars Anderson, a Bay Area outfielder.

Brett Anderson (unrelated to Lars) was one of them. Shawn Tolleson was another. So was Grant Green, who had just hit.455 as a junior in Anaheim. Marcus Lemon, a shortstop from Orlando whose father was All-Star outfielder Chet Lemon, batted.489 as a junior. Max Sapp, a powerful catcher, has competed in international events since the age of thirteen. The studs conducted themselves "like gods on a baseball field," according to Lars Anderson.

Kershaw grew in importance to some of the mortals as the trials progressed. Dwight Childs, like Anderson, Kershaw, and so many of the lads in Joplin, was nervous. Childs, a Bay Area catcher, regained confidence after fouling off a Kershaw fastball down the third base line. "Then he threw me the nastiest curve—I swear to God this thing touched the clouds and came back down to my knees," Childs told me afterwards. "I've never seen a curveball like this. I don't believe anyone had, at this point."

Kershaw's brilliance, however, was only rare. During the trials, Brett Anderson warmed up beside Team USA head coach Jerry Dawson. Anderson's positioning was so exact that he apologized to his catcher for missing his position. "And he only missed it by a foot," Dawson recounted. "Wherever you put it, it was there." Kershaw couldn't. "He was good," said Brandon Belt, a left-handed pitcher from Lufkin, Texas. "But he wasn't like the Clayton Kershaw everybody knows now." Dawson thought his delivery was hurried, with his legs lurching forward before his left arm was ready. "At that point, he was having trouble throwing strikes," Dawson told me. "But the stuff was above and beyond."

Dawson was a highly decorated high school coach in America. He had attended Chaparral High School in Scottsdale, Arizona, for over 30 years. Chaparral has won the state championship five out of the previous seven years. "He was a ball of fire," said L. V. Ware is an outfielder from Atlanta. Dawson pays close care to appearance. He outlawed eye black, sunglasses on cap bills, and gloves swinging from pockets. He debated cutting Dellin Betances, a six-foot-eight New Yorker who wore his cap sideways, but ultimately relented. Dawson had helped the national team the previous year. In 2005, he was joined by Hisey, a former minor leaguer and pitching coach at Pima Community College in Tucson. The coaches designed a pitching lineup for the competition in Mexico. They determined that Anderson should lead the rotation. Tyson Ross, a six-foot-five right-handed pitcher from Oakland, was up next. He was a month older than Kershaw, but one grade higher. He had left freshman orientation at the University of California, Berkeley, to attend the trials. Ross had previously played for Team USA in the summer, alongside future All-Stars Andrew McCutchen, Buster Posey, and Justin Upton. "Brett Anderson and Tyson were dominant," Ware explained.

Betances, Kershaw, and Josh Thrailkill, a right-handed North Carolina pitcher, completed the rotation. Tolleson loomed as a multi-inning relief option. Officials from Team USA could not picture Kershaw in a comparable capacity. They had watched his pre-game routine. It was a 45-minute ceremony that was meticulously detailed but difficult to execute. "Because we can't do all this rigmarole, coming into the sixth inning," Darwin chuckled.

After a week in Joplin, USA Baseball authorities reduced the roster to forty. Those forty played another week of games. That group shrank to twenty-six. The athletes split among California, Miami, and Texas. In late August, the squad regrouped in Cobb County, Georgia, just north of Atlanta. There was another round of games versus local children and Team Canada. Following that, Team USA selected their twenty-man roster. The team took the bus to the Atlanta airport. Kershaw had taken a few flights in his life. He was leaving the country for the first time, but in a strangely familiar role: he was one of America's top pitchers. However, other boys performed better.

A police escort met Team USA at Villahermosa International Airport. The early September heat seemed stifling as the players boarded buses destined for Villahermosa, Tabasco's capital, on the Gulf of Mexico. At the motel, children battered the bus's sides. Dawson advised the players to sign autographs only for children, not adults. The opening ceremony at Estadio Centenario was a rowdy event. Several players claimed to see police holding AK-47s and AR-15s atop the dugouts. "Like, 'Am I with the Beatles right now?'" recalls Lars Anderson.

The environment provided more problems to Americans than most of their opponents. USA Baseball officials were concerned that rebels might ignore Dawson's curfew. They were concerned about rain disturbing the schedule. And, of course, "you're always fighting the food battle when you go to those places," Hisey said. This was well before the days of meal planning and meticulous dieting. Team USA ate chips and salsa for breakfast. After the games, they ate Domino's pizza, which was delivered to their hotel by a person on a moped with a heater on the back. A few people took advantage of the drinking age, which was eighteen. Others dabbled in more mundane activities. Tolleson drank Fanta "like it was water," he said. Kershaw, Tolleson, and Brett Anderson went outside the hotel for street tacos. They were able to avoid the batches that had been causing problems for their teammates. "Oh my gosh, the street tacos just wrecked you," said Greg Peavey, a pitcher from Portland's suburbs. "They were fine going down. And then, about an hour later, you were done." The gastrointestinal distress was not limited to athletes. "I lived the last four or five days of that tournament on Imodium, pretty much," recalls Hisey. By the end, Darwin's jars of peanut butter and jelly provided sustenance for the majority of the traveling party.

The conditions were not optimal. Dawson took one afternoon batting practice behind a chain-link L-screen. The grass at one location looked "like it hadn't been cut in years," Ware recalled. To prepare the field after a rainy afternoon, stadium personnel hauled gasoline canisters and set the home plate on fire. The flames helped dry the grass. "And immediately, it was like, 'Play ball!'" Tolleson recalls. "I was like, 'We should remember that.'"

Kershaw tagged along with Tolleson "like a puppy dog," Darwin said. They passed the time by kicking the Hacky Sack with Anderson and reading the Bible. They discussed what they may accomplish in the Big 12 after graduation, despite the fact that all three planned to enter the first round rather than attend college. Kershaw understood why their ambitions appeared more realistic than his own. When he witnessed Anderson's positioning and Tolleson's dominance, he identified areas where he could improve. "I always played with guys who were better than me," Kershaw explained. "I believe that's good. At the end of the day, it's okay not to be the best all the time.

During the first week of the event, he witnessed his peers dominate the competition. Dawson planned his rotation such that Anderson and Ross would be available for the finals. Kershaw took fourth place. He spent time in the bullpen. The boys ripped farts and made jokes. Tolleson entertained the gang with his double-jointed elbows. "I think we lit someone's cleat on fire," Childs said.

The rain wiped off Kershaw's start versus Brazil. The game was postponed for three days. Kershaw lasted just four innings. He allowed three hits and walked four batters. The story was the same as throughout the trials. He threw with a three-quarters arm angle, straining his elbow. His delivery lacked consistency. Sometimes everything clicked into place. At other instances, his body moved too fast. He appeared nervous when compared to Anderson, who struck out 24 of the 50 hitters he faced throughout the tournament. Anderson gave up an early run against Panama the day following Kershaw's start. In the dugout, Anderson flung his glove against the wall and unleashed "probably fifteen of the most beautifully strung together profanities you could ever ask to hear from anybody," Dawson remembered. Dawson said to his hitting coach, "If you can score two runs, this game is over." Team USA scored seven runs. Panama didn't score again.

Kershaw saw Ross begin the gold medal game against Cuba from the bullpen. Team USA has not lost the competition. The group had defeated Cuba a week before. However, late in the game, the Cubans picked off a runner at second base and then scored the go-ahead run when they came up to bat. Dawson was expelled. He was never certain why. The linguistic barrier didn't help. (It should be mentioned that Dawson had a natural dislike for umpires: "I despise them all," stated Dawson, who was still coaching at Yavapai College in Prescott, Arizona, in 2023.)

The Americans were defeated 2-1. The setback hit the adults the hardest. The athletes were eager to get back to the States with memories and souvenirs. Following the game, the Americans exchanged gear with the Cubans. More than a decade later, Tolleson and Ware still had Team Cuba jackets hanging in their wardrobe. Most of the players returned to their hotel. A few people breached the curfew one last time. The next morning, at the airport, Darwin wished them wisdom gained from youthful hangovers. Back home, school had already started. Ross would start his first year at Berkeley. The majority would be high school seniors: Kershaw in Highland Park, Anderson in Stillwater, and Tolleson in Allen. They were filled with curiosity about what the coming year would bring, as well as the years after that.

CHAPTER 3
A SEASON OF DEFINING MOMENTS

*T*he Dallas Morning News published a preseason report outlining the stakes for Clayton Kershaw's final season at Highland Park. The team had a chance to advance to the state tournament, and Kershaw had the opportunity to break Xerxes Martin's school record of thirty-one career victories. He was descended from Highland Park pitchers Martin, Zane Carlson, and San Diego Padres starter Chris Young. Kershaw, writes Tim MacMahon, "might be the best of them all." Kershaw told MacMahon he aspired to turn pro: "If it's the right situation, I wouldn't hesitate."

Early that spring, Kershaw and Patrick Halpin played catch at Scotland Yard. Halpin knew his friend had played baseball all throughout North America that summer, and he also knew Kershaw had taken pitching lessons in the winter. The progress was disguised until Kershaw reared back and fired.

"I could tell that something was different," Halpin recalled. "In our little long-toss warmups, he was throwing it on a rope from the center-field wall."

The contrast was much more apparent during Kershaw's bullpens. His fastball no longer hovered in the upper 80s. "Somebody gets a gun out there, like, 'Oh, my God, this is like 89 mph, touching 90, 91 every now and then,'" Halpin told me. "All of a sudden, it's like, 93 to 95 mph."

Before leaving for spring training with the Padres, Young went to his alma mater, his six-foot-ten frame visible in the spectators as he watched Kershaw pitch. "I could tell how electric the ball was," Young explained. In Allen, Shawn Tolleson began to hear rumors.

He watched a game at Highland Park, amazed at his friend: "I was like, 'Wow, what happened to you in one winter?'"

Clayton Kershaw's senior season at Highland Park High unfurled like a dream when viewed from a distance, with the dual amplifying perspectives of hindsight and nostalgia.

He never missed a start. Skip Johnson's changes devastated opposition hitters. "My senior year, I don't know if there was a time that I threw harder in my life," Kershaw told me. His numbers were astonishing. He finished with an ERA of 0.77. He struck out almost two batters per inning. He pitched a perfect game, striking out all hitters. He progressed from interesting arm to fringe first-rounder to a guy worth considering by the team with the first overall choice. He made Mark Lummus's claim about his place in Texas history seem plausible.

However, it was also a year in which Kershaw dealt with questions about his performance, health, and finances. The pressure, which had been building since he was a freshman, only increased. This isn't just a game anymore, he remembered thinking. This might be my future. When he rose to prominence in the major leagues, his preference for starter turkey sandwiches was funny. The reason Kershaw went to the local shop New York Sub for pregame lunches was more fundamental. "A turkey sandwich is the easiest thing to eat," he said. His anxiety suppressed his appetite. He stumbled through the halls in a stupor on his first day, which was usually a Friday evening. "I had to go to class and take tests and quizzes, and I was like, 'Golly, I don't want to be here,'" he remembers.

The majority of his friends and teammates only saw what he projected: John Wayne on the mound, a buffoon off it. Some of his close friends were aware of his financial difficulties. "My mom had borrowed money from my friend's parents," Kershaw recounted. "Which sucks, right?" The experience had an impact on his psychology. "They would have to ask people for things," Ellen recounted. "And I believe Clayton, even at a young age, felt a sense of shame and apprehension about never repaying them.'" Kershaw realized that the loans would have to be returned with any money he earned in the draft. "I knew I'd have to help," he explained. "But I didn't realize the extent of how much it was."

Clayton Kershaw's senior season at Highland Park High played out like a dream—and also as a glimpse into the future. That season marked the first time Kershaw fully embraced the responsibility of greatness. The weight would remain there for the rest of his professional life.

"I think that's where all the nerves and pressure came," he told me. "It meant a lot."

Deric Ladnier, scouting director for the Kansas City Royals, who own the first overall pick in the draft, stood on the bleachers above the Highland Park bullpen, staring down at Clayton Kershaw. On a wet day in Dallas, the image before him was vivid. The fastball crackled with energy. However, it did not always arrive where the catcher had positioned the mitt. The curveball was captivating. But occasionally it bounced. "He was not an elite strike thrower," Ladnier said. "But he was an elite stuff guy." Ladnier observed Kershaw's delivery, the 1-2-3 movement that could be so mesmerizing, and speculated on where it might go wrong.

The Royals were in disarray, heading for another hundred-loss season. The squad hadn't made the playoffs since 1985. On May 31, one week before the draft, owner David Glass opted to replace general manager Allard Baird with Braves executive Dayton Moore. Ladnier remained in control of the proceedings. His duty needed him to choose a player who could help the big league club in the near future.

Kershaw's reward was evident. However, there was a risk.

The MLB draft is significantly more volatile than the NFL and NBA drafts. In those sports, if a top pick flops, the guilty organization faces a lifetime of humiliation. Ryan Leaf and Darko Miličić have become household names. In 1998, Jeff Austin (MLB's No. 4 overall pick) and Kyle Sleeth (No. 3 pick in 2003, when the Detroit Pistons picked Miličić over Carmelo Anthony) were relatively unknown. Amateur baseball players' developmental paths were less linear than in other sports: injuries were prevalent, the professional schedule was more demanding, and young players had to learn to adjust to failure. The process was difficult to foresee.

No athlete was more volatile than a high school pitcher.

From 1996 to 2000, twelve high school pitchers were drafted in the top ten. Nine never made it to the majors. Josh Beckett, the No. 2 overall pick in 1999 who led the Florida Marlins to the 2003 World Series, was an exception. The rule applies to flameouts such as Geoff Goetz, Josh Girdley, and Bobby Bradley. Many analysts argued that selecting a high school pitcher so early in the draft was akin to putting millions of dollars in a barrel and dropping a match. Four prep pitchers were selected in the first round of the 2002 draft and went on to become All Stars. However, as evaluators wrote reports for the 2006 draft, the success of the three pitchers taken ahead of that quartet served as a caution. Cincinnati had drafted California righty Chris Gruler at No. 3. Next, Baltimore selected Adam Loewen, a Canadian right-hander. Clint Everts of Texas was selected as the fifth pick by Montreal. Only a few years later, they all looked like busts. "If you get the right one, they usually end up being stars," Ladnier explained. "But the probability of getting the right one is very slim."

Ladnier had only acquired one of the appropriate ones a few years ago. Baird was looking for a collegiate pitcher in spring 2002, according to Ladnier. After seeing Zack Greinke, a preternaturally polished right-hander from the Orlando suburbs, Ladnier informed his employer, "You're getting one. He's only 18 years old." Ladnier was unable to provide the same promise on Kershaw. Greinke repeated his delivery with metronomic accuracy. "It was like watching Greg Maddux pitch in high school," Ladnier remarked. What about Kershaw, though? Ladnier was unsure whether he'd throw enough strikes. The attraction of the other pitchers in the selection was considerable.

The new class of college pitchers appeared to be among the greatest in recent memory. Andrew Miller, an imposing lefty from the University of North Carolina, received the Roger Clemens Award, college baseball's version of the Cy Young. The other contenders included University of Houston lefty Brad Lincoln, who earned the Dick Howser Award for collegiate player of the year. Tim Lincecum, a slender dynamo from the University of Washington, won the Golden Spikes Award.

Even gamers without hardware were impressed. Stanford righty Greg Reynolds wowed scouts with his six-foot-seven physique. Brandon Morrow, a right-handed pitcher from the University of California, Berkeley, "had one of the best true arms I've ever seen on a kid," Mariners scouting director Bob Fontaine said. Max Scherzer, a belligerent right-hander who predominantly threw fastballs, starred at the University of Missouri. Miller's Tar Heel teammate Daniel Bard was also present, as were Ian Kennedy of the University of Southern California and Joba Chamberlain of the University of Nebraska.

Luke Hochevar was pitching for an independent squad in Fort Worth. A year ago, he expected to sign with the Dodgers. His saga was the first domino in a chain reaction that resulted in Clayton Kershaw falling into Logan White's lap. It was the type of sequence that reinforces a man's faith in the divine. "To me," White remembered, "it was all part of God's plan that he be there."

Kershaw established his new position in the baseball scene one afternoon in May. He was at a friend's house when he discovered the May 8-21 issue of Baseball America. The magazine promised "Big Changes" for its pre-draft rankings. The most significant change was that Kershaw had risen to become the nation's top high school prospect. "I was like, 'Oh, that's cool,'" he said.

The vagaries of the game destroyed his friends and peers, causing injuries, ineffectiveness, and aesthetic bias. Jordan Walden strained a groin muscle earlier this year. He opted to continue pitching. His velocity decreased, as did his opinion of his prospects. Brett Anderson was subjected to the harsh scrutiny of professional scouts. As a senior, he stood six feet four and weighed 215 pounds. Evaluators questioned his athleticism. The balletic perfection with which he delivered his message was less important than the puffiness on his face. Scouts lowered his ceiling.

Shawn Tolleson suffered the most severe consequences. Kershaw and Tolleson had taken parallel courses. Tolleson made the varsity team at Allen as a freshman and profited from the experience before his physique matured. He dedicated his summers to baseball. He studied swings on the diamond and Bibles away from it. He even committed to Baylor for the same reason Kershaw chose Texas A&M: Tolleson's girlfriend, Lynley, was a student there. Tolleson, like Kershaw, refused to go to campus. He discussed his future frequently with his parents. His father had a prosperous veterinary practice. Tolleson's valued education. Tolleson had a burning desire to play baseball. They agreed to a compromise before the season began. If Shawn was chosen in the early rounds, his parents would allow him to turn professional. "And so in my head, I was like, Got to be a first rounder, I've got to be a first rounder," Tolleson told ESPN.

When spring arrived, Tolleson felt he had a chance. Twenty-five scouts attended his first scrimmage. An even larger audience gathered to watch Allen face the Woodlands, a suburban Houston powerhouse. Tolleson faced off against Kyle Drabek, a projected first-round pick. "That," remembered Paul Goldschmidt, the Woodlands' third baseman, "was a big game." In the third inning, Tolleson felt an alarming crack in his elbow while throwing a slider. In his heart, he knew what had occurred. But he didn't want to alarm the scouts. He pointed at his ankle. Tolleson, in his final act as a high school pitcher, faked a limp as he left the field, hoping to trick the evaluators.

The ruse was revealed a few days later. An examination indicated that Tolleson had injured his ulnar collateral ligament. He required Tommy John surgery. His senior year was over. His first-round hopes were shattered. "We all make plans in our life that never work out how we think they're going to work out," Tolleson told me. He eventually came to see this as a blessing. At the time, he felt only sadness.

"I felt bad for him," Kershaw explained. "I felt really bad for him." He also believed that, despite the setback, Tolleson would be fine. "Shawn came from a good family," Kershaw explained. "And it wasn't, like, going to make or break his life, getting drafted." Kershaw did not have the same luxury.

Marianne and Clayton, like potential advisors earlier this year, invited big-league officials to their home during the season. Chris Kershaw remained on the fringe, occasionally questioning scouts about his son but not attending at-home visits. The sector could pave the way for an imperfect family life. Kershaw refused to sugarcoat him. "He acknowledged that it wasn't an ideal situation," Lummus recalled. "He made it very clear it wasn't the end of the world, in his eyes."

Marianne never asked for money, Lummus recalled. She pelted him with questions, including where Clayton would reside. Who managed the transportation? How would the team track him during the winter? When Diamondbacks scout Trip Couch saw Kershaw pitch, he said, "What's not to like about this guy?" A visit to the Kershaw home reaffirmed his passion. "They lived in a smaller home there in Highland Park," Couch said. "I just remember being blown away about what a great kid this was."

Not every team created that impression. Kershaw retained fragments from the meetings. A Florida Marlins scout chastised him for wearing shorts and a t-shirt. "He was like, 'It's a bad representation of who you are,'" Kershaw explained. "And I was like, 'No, this is who I am.' Some of those guys were just stupid." In a meeting with the Pittsburgh Pirates, who had the No. 4 choice, he answered a question about the infield fly rule. "I said, 'I know what that is. Why do you care?Kershaw recalled.

Kershaw expected Pittsburgh to grab him. The team had emailed him a series of questions, which was a normal practice at the time. His eyes glazed over during the questionnaire. "Probably toward the end of them, I was just, like, click, click, click," he says. At the meeting, the Pirates informed him that he had failed the exam. They feared he wasn't competitive enough. "They said I had conflicting answers," Kershaw explained. "Sorry. What do you want me to do? I am not going to retake it."

The Dodgers chose a different approach. White never went to the Kershaw residence. He did not speak with Clayton or Marianne. Aside from one brief talk with Chris Kershaw, he avoided touch with his family. "The last thing I need to do is create attention," White said, lest the six teams drafting ahead of him wonder why the Dodgers were so excited about this adolescent with an unusual delivery. Calvin Jones made a quick home pitch. After exchanging pleasantries, he inquired whether Kershaw would sign if the Dodgers selected him in the first round. Kershaw said he would. Jones thanked the family for their time and departed. Kershaw thought that the encounter lasted about five minutes. "I was like, 'Wow, you guys get it,'" he explained.

J. D. Smart attempted to prepare Kershaw for the financial implications of his situation. "How much would you be willing to sign for?" Smart inquired one afternoon over burgers at a neighborhood establishment named Chips. "Not much," Kershaw replied. "Enough to cover this lunch," he explained. Smart revealed how much money Kershaw could get if he went in the first round: $1.5 million. Kershaw felt his eyes well up. The sum astounded him. "I was like, 'Oh my, that's fantastic. Take it!'" He recalled.

Kershaw's advisors did their own reconnaissance. Alan Hendricks contacted Logan White. They had a normal conversation for that time of year, two seasoned gentlemen looking for information while keeping it casual and toeing the line between honesty and caginess.

There was no reason to assume Kershaw would stay that long, at least until his April 28 start against Forney. In the second inning, he felt a stretch in his left side. Six weeks before the most important event of his life, Kershaw had done something he believed he could not afford to do. He got harmed.

For three weeks, Kershaw did not pitch. The damage was minor; he had pulled an oblique muscle, or "chublique," as he later described it. But the layoff was lengthy enough to instill hope in Mark Lummus. He questioned if the injury would deter other clubs and force the kid to slide to Seattle's second-round choice at No. 49. He was curious to see how Kershaw would react when he returned to play on May 19.

The Scots hosted Northwest, a high school in Justin some 35 miles west, in the Class 4A regional quarterfinal. Texans coach Che Hendrix hoped that a rigorous pitch count would limit his usage. The first inning raised Hendrix's expectations. Kershaw was rusty and rushed, mindful of the scouts, the stakes, and the potential cost of a hiccup in the hundreds of thousands of dollars. He stuck to fastballs. The Texans committed numerous fouls. All three at-bats resulted in strikeouts, though they took a while. "I'm not sure if he threw a ball the rest of the game," Hendrix said.

Kershaw struck out the side in the second inning. By the third, Hendrix's optimism had evaporated. His sons were being swamped. They still hadn't placed the ball in play. He stormed out of the dugout to reprimand the umpire.

"Everything can't be a strike," Hendrix explained.

The umpire insisted, "Coach, I've never seen anything like it. Everything is a strike."

Hendrix deflated. "God dang it," he exclaimed. "That's what I figured."

Kershaw struck out everyone in the third inning. He struck out the entire fourth inning. In the bottom of the inning, he hit a home run. Then he returned to striking everyone out. Highland Park triggered the ten-run mercy rule in the fifth inning, which halted the game. This left Kershaw's line clean and absurd: a five-inning perfect game. He faced 15 hitters and struck them all out. He had put an end to any concerns about his health, as well as any possibility of remaining available in the second round.

In the days leading up to the Class 4A Region II semifinal at Dr Pepper Ballpark in Frisco, the home of the Rangers' double-A club, Corsicana coach Tracy Wood rehearsed a mantra regarding the forthcoming opponent. "When you're on deck, start swinging," Wood said. Before the first pitch, Corsicana junior Stayton Thomas attempted to time the heater. He believed that was his only opportunity. Thomas had admired Kershaw from a distance while playing for the age group behind him at D-Bat. "We knew he was about to become a millionaire," Thomas recounted.

Depending on who you believe, Thomas may have reduced Kershaw's initial bonus. Kershaw was shaky at the start. Thomas followed Wood's advice, ignoring the curveball and waiting for a full-count fastball. Kershaw complied. Thomas was ready. He rocketed the ball past the 364-foot marker in left center field. This wouldn't be another perfect game. Corsicana pursued Kershaw all evening. So did their fans. He heard the famous phrase "O-ver-rated!" chants. His bat protected his arm. He singled to tie the game in the second inning then homered in the fourth. Kershaw picked off a runner to get out of a fourth-inning jam. Highland Park won by 8-3.

Logan White was undeterred by the shakiness. "Clayton's such a competitor, when you tell him, 'Oh, you didn't throw as good in that game,' he gets pissed at me," White remembers. "But I'm like, 'Clayton, don't be furious. I know the scouts. I know what people saw." Over the years, Dodgers scouts relayed stories about where Pirates executives were that evening. Some reported that Pirates general manager Dave Littlefield was in Houston, watching Brad Lincoln destroy East Carolina. Others remembered him in Frisco, where Kershaw struggled to place his curveball. White recalls taunting John Green, a Pirates scout who shared his admiration for Kershaw, at the airport the next day. "Greeny!"White said. Nice game to have your guy at."

(I contacted Littlefield in October 2022. "I received your email," he replied. "Nothing personal, but I'll pass on the conversation." I tried to reach Pirates scouting director Ed Creech; a person identifying himself as Creech's son responded and indicated his father, now in his seventies, was "retired and not too interested in discussing baseball lately." Green did not respond to a message.)

The story became part of Dodger scouting history. But Thomas had never heard about the alleged significance of his home run. When I told him, he cackled on the phone. "I apologize, Mr. Kershaw and family," said Thomas, who played in the minor leagues for Tampa

Bay before becoming a high school coach. "But I guess you're welcome, Dodgers fans."

Two days after Thomas went deep but Corsicana went home, three coaches from McKinney North, a school approximately 30 minutes from Highland Park, drove south on US Route 75. They stopped at a McDonald's beside the freeway. Brandon Milam collected his assistants and headed inside to see Scots' head coach, Lew Kennedy.

The aroma of breakfast encompassed them: egg McMuffins and sausage biscuits, pancakes with fake syrup, family gathering after church. "Everybody else is enjoying their coffee and we're sweating bullets," Milam told me afterwards. The two teams were unable to agree on the rules of their scheduled match. The rules provided a choice between a one-game or three-game series. Kennedy preferred a one-game playoff with Kershaw on the mound. Milam requested three games. They settled it in the same way that they did in Texas. They flipped the coin. (A week before, Kennedy had encountered Wood, the Corsicana coach, at a gas station. "Well," Wood replied after losing the toss, "it's been a good year."

Back in McKinney, Milam's wife, Lesley, had urged her Sunday school pupils to pray about the throw. Her husband took out his lucky quarter. He gave it to one of his assistants, Brooke Court. He asked his other assistant, Ricky Carter, to make the call.

"Tails never fails," Carter remarked.

Court flipped the coin. Heads symbolized destruction, a one-night stand against the finest pitcher in the country. Tails represented redemption in a series that gave McKinney North a chance. The coin clattered off the table and onto the floor. The coaches slipped beneath the booth to await the verdict.

Tails.

The McKinney North coaches were thrilled. Milam's gears spun. He had two excellent pitchers: Trent Appleby, a junior going for Texas Christian University, and Michael Bolsinger, a senior who had previously played for D-Bat. The familiarity led to overconfidence. "I want Kershaw," Bolsinger informed the coaches. Milam shot him down. He had a better idea.

On May 31, 2006, Clayton Kershaw relaxed on the Dr Pepper Ballpark outfield. He worked through his pregame stretching routine for what may be his final amateur debut. On the other side of the diamond, deception was afoot.

Milam carried two lineup cards: one if Kershaw pitched and another if he did not. Milam instructed Appleby to warm up. Milam expected Kershaw to start, but he kept an eye on the opposing bullpen to make sure. When Kershaw picked up a ball, Milam activated a seldom-used sophomore named Bryan Kinard, who had been notified of his assignment earlier in the week. "Coach Milan came up to me, and he was like, 'Oh, hey, by the way, you got the first game,'" Kinard told me. "And I simply said, 'Hold up. What?'" The young man took on a sacrifice role. Milam planned to save Appleby and Bolsinger for the next two games. Highland Park scored six runs in the top of the first. Kershaw failed to nail his curveball for strikes yet again. He walked four in five innings, but Highland Park won 13-1 after using the five-inning mercy rule.

Kershaw would never pitch as an amateur again. Milam's plan worked. McKinney North won the following two games. Kershaw considered the conclusion of a chapter. Josh, Patrick, and the rest of the lads were headed to college. Kershaw was waiting for the draft, unsure of his next step and saddened that his senior year had ended. Kershaw felt humbled when McKinney North spilled out of its dugout to cheer, knowing that his team should have advanced. He saw a dogpile form on the diamond. The scene would become frighteningly familiar.

CHAPTER 4
DRAFTING SEASON

*T*Logan White Jr.'s father revealed his plan to his son on June 5, 2006, two days after his eighth birthday and one day before the Major League Baseball Rule 4 draft. All those hours spent imagining the future, all those miles in rental cars, all those nights in inexpensive Marriotts—they all pointed to this moment. White illustrated the scenery for his son. He wanted Clayton Kershaw. There were multiple teams in the way. He had heard that the Detroit Tigers, who picked one spot ahead of the Dodgers, were conflicted between Kershaw and Andrew Miller, a left-handed pitcher from the University of North Carolina. However, Kansas City may spend the No. 1 overall pick on Miller. So White requested a favor: "When you go to bed tonight and say your prayers, say a prayer that Clayton can get to us."

The following morning, friends flocked into Kershaw's house. Ellen arrived with her parents. About a dozen people arrived, including Chris. As the Kershaws waited for the draft to begin, Dodgers officials met in a conference room at Dodger Stadium. Kershaw ranked first on the department's board. The only other player White considered was Evan Longoria, a third baseman for Long Beach State. However, White did not expect Longoria to fall outside the top five.

If Kershaw was not available, White did not plan to look into college pitching. Scott Boras, who handled the disastrous negotiations with Luke Hochevar, represented Max Scherzer, the University of Missouri's right-handed pitcher. White also ruled out Tim Lincecum, the University of Washington's lithe, electrifying pitcher. Earlier this summer, White urged Dodgers executive Roy Smith to scout Lincecum. Smith admired Lincecum's talent but was concerned about how he might age. "I feel the same way," White said.

Several days before the draft, White invited another pitcher to Dodger Stadium. Bryan Morris, a right-handed pitcher from Tennessee, had spent the season at a local minor college. "You're not supposed to have pre-draft deals," White explained. "But if you word it a certain way, it's fine." White devised a backup strategy using some deft linguistics. White may spend $2.3 million on the No. 7 pick. Morris was prepared to sign for $1.8 million. If Kershaw was selected in the top six, White decided that the Dodgers would take Morris and shift the funds elsewhere.

White communicated the prospective $500,000 discount to Ned Colletti. There was a discussion regarding the benefits of saving money. White was stumped for selecting Kershaw. (Colletti claimed he didn't recall a dispute.) They reached an accord. If Kershaw were present, he would be a Dodger.

But will he be there?

In 2006, another distinction emerged between the MLB draft and its counterparts in the NFL and NBA. It was not televised. Executives followed a basic online broadcast. They worked the phones, contacting agents, players, and colleagues. Tim Hallgren, a Dodgers scout, was related to other teams. His canvassing generated hope. It came from an unusual source: Hochevar, the Dodger who never existed.

Kershaw had already been ruled out by the Royals earlier this spring. "As much as I don't like to admit it, Clayton would not have been a factor for us in picking No. 1 in the country," scouting director Deric Ladnier said. They deliberated between Hochevar and Miller. When the Royals chose Hochevar, the Dodgers gained an advantage: the Tigers would have to choose between Miller and Kershaw. The executives were well aware that the better bet was nearly always on the college arm.

The following few picks went White's way. Colorado selected six-foot-seven Stanford righty Greg Reynolds, whose career would be hampered by shoulder issues. R. J. Harrison was selected third for the Tampa Bay Devil Rays. Harrison scouted Kershaw twice. He observed the same things that Ladnier saw: attraction and instability. He chose Longoria, who earned the American League Rookie of the Year award in 2008 as the team transformed into a low-budget success. "There are some times you wake up in the middle of the night, in a cold sweat, wondering why you did something that didn't work out well," Harrison told me. "In this case, I don't lose too much sleep." Because we chose a guy who became the face of our franchise for ten years. As a scouting director, I've probably never made a better choice."

The Pirates couldn't say the same. Kevin McClatchy, the owner, preferred college players over high schoolers, which constrained general manager Dave Littlefield. "Dave wasn't going to be able to take a high school pitcher," said a source acquainted with the matter. Pittsburgh chose Brad Lincoln, a University of Houston pitcher. Later in life, Kershaw reflected on his good fortune to avoid Pittsburgh. "I remember pitching one game and my curveball wasn't good, so that was, like, the final straw from them," he told me. "That's great. "I am glad I am not there."

The Mariners were up next. Mark Lummus' early insights did not outweigh the dictates of ownership. Bob Fontaine Jr., the scouting director, chose Brandon Morrow, a pitcher from California. Lummus was torn about his decision. But he understood. "He did the right thing," Lummus remembered.

The dominoes had fallen just as White had desired. Only Detroit stood between Kershaw and the Dodgers. "If Andrew Miller hadn't been there, Clayton Kershaw wouldn't have been a Dodger," former

Tigers general manager Dave Dombrowski said. But Miller was there, in part because Hochevar had not signed the previous year.

Six teams had a chance to acquire Kershaw. All six passed. The seventh wouldn't.

A tiny amount of drama remained. White used a timeout, which was an option back then, to freeze the clock for five minutes so he could negotiate with Hendricks about a piece of contractual jargon that Dodgers owner Frank McCourt required and agents despised—a clause mandating a player to repay his bonus if he left the sport. Gary Nickels remained on the phone with a Dodgers employee posted beside the fax machine. When the documentation arrived, Nickels indicated to White. They were good to go. Clayton Kershaw, a left-handed pitcher from Highland Park High School in Dallas, was taken seventh overall in the 2006 MLB draft by the Dodgers.

Moments later, Marianne Kershaw's landline called.

The phone rang for a while. When Kershaw received the news, he raised his arms in the air. The Texas A&M coach, Rob Childress, called to say his best recruit farewell. Cade Griffis, the D-Bat's owner, overheard Kershaw's voice crack on the phone. Kershaw accepted a few more calls and received some backslaps and high fives. "A lot of happy tears," Patrick Halpin remembered. Kershaw then celebrated with his friends: despite being a blossoming millionaire, he couldn't beat his pals in Halo.

The happiness was only momentary. Kershaw's first professional contract with the Dodgers was a $2.3 million bonus. He believed he was financially secure for life. He felt briefly relieved. It didn't last long. He couldn't believe how much he needed to pay his agency. Then he needed to settle his mother's debts. Marianne had borrowed approximately $15,000 over the years from the parents of her son's pals, according to Kershaw. Clayton repaid the money. However, the loans had strained these connections. Some of them fractured. Marianne still had bills to pay. His father also pleaded for assistance. Relief gave way to reality.

Kershaw felt something solidify as a result of his tension. He had worked hard to achieve this goal, which was to save the draft. He had achieved his goal. Kershaw was chosen first out of all the lads that played high school baseball in 2006. The draft strengthened Kershaw's faith in God's providence. "That was when my faith started getting stronger, when I saw the fruits of that," he remembers. However, he had not resolved all of his family's issues.

Now, he told himself, I need to make it to the major leagues.

Because Kershaw signed so quickly, the Dodgers wanted him to start pitching before the minor league season was over. That summer, the franchise educated him into its corporate culture. Two weeks after the draft, he was scheduled to fly to Los Angeles.

As his leaving date approached, Kershaw was scrambling. "I didn't have a suitcase," he explained. Leslie Melson arrived at his residence with goods and said, "Didn't have anything." She bought him new socks, underwear, deodorant, and toiletries. She packed them in a fresh set of luggage. The Melsons purchased Kershaw a laptop so he could communicate with Ellen. Leslie handed him some cash in case he needed it. "I don't know what I would have done without Ellen's parents packing me, basically," Kershaw said afterwards. The remembrance caused Jim Melson to blink back tears. "Leslie was the epitome of a mother," he said.

Kershaw bid goodbye to Marianne and his buddies. He wasn't sure when he'd be home. Ellen was on her way to Texas A&M for summer studies, and they planned to reconnect whenever they could. Then he stepped out of his upbringing and took a plane to the West Coast.

A whirlwind awaited him. In Los Angeles, he met another of the team's adolescent first-round picks, Preston Mattingly, the son of former Yankees player Don Mattingly. The two discovered professionals shared a ride to Dodger Stadium. They visited the clubhouse and the offices. They met Tommy Lasorda, the Hall of Fame manager, and Vin Scully, the famed announcer. Kershaw sat with Colletti, the mustachioed Chicagoan who oversaw the team's baseball operations. Kershaw wore a clean Dodgers jersey over a baggy blue button-down when being introduced before a game. Mattingly gaped as he listened to Kershaw's statistics. "I remember looking over and saying, 'Oh my God.'" Who is this guy?Mattingly recalled.

The teenagers took another flight. Kershaw and Mattingly had been assigned to the Dodgers' lowest-level domestic club, the Gulf Coast League, on Florida's east coast. When they arrived, they hopped in a van and drove to Vero Beach, a peaceful hamlet. They drove past palm trees before pulling into a parking area. Kershaw had a wish in his heart and a goal in his mind: he wanted to make it to the majors by his twenty-first birthday. The first step occurred when he got out of the van and stepped into Dodgertown.

Branch Rickey created the establishment. In the late 1940s, Rickey, the Brooklyn Dodgers' president, was looking for a training facility. Bud Holman showed him an abandoned World War II naval base a few hours north of Miami.

"There among palms, palmettos, scrub pines, and swamp," Roger Kahn wrote in The Boys of Summer.

Rickey commissioned the construction of baseball diamonds, batting cages, and sliding pits. Bullpen mounds sprouted throughout the property. The barracks accommodated the whole crew. Rickey had developed the current farm system, and the spring training complex was another innovation. It was a baseball utopia in principle, but black players were nevertheless subjected to Jim Crow's degradations. Jackie's wife, Rachel Robinson, told Kahn about being prevented from shopping with the white women. Kahn once asked pitcher Joe Black, a Black man from New Jersey, what he thought about spring training in the South. "I can't tell you," Black replied. "They won't let me in."

Dodgertown's legacy was checkered. However, it remained a vital component of the franchise's structure. "Walking around Dodgertown," former Dodgers prospect Wesley Wright recalled, "it's like walking into history." Inside the Championship Hall, a mural of World Series rings welcomed visitors: "Six Dodger World Championship teams began here!On an adjacent wall, the champions were listed: 1955, 1959, 1963, 1965, 1981, and 1988." Young hitters such as Mattingly used the same diamonds as Robinson, Pee Wee Reese, and Duke Snider formerly did. Young pitchers like Kershaw followed in the footsteps of Sandy Koufax, Don Drysdale, and Don Sutton. "You just think about all the greats who have been on that same field," former Dodgers prospect James McDonald said. By the time Kershaw and Mattingly came, the town was beginning to show its age. Kershaw spotted old street signs and no traffic as he drove out from the airport. He was entering an isolated, sheltered environment.

Kershaw shared a room with Kyle Smit, a tiny fifth-round pick from just outside Reno, Nevada. Smit was a quiet child who felt overwhelmed by the transition. He had never spent much time alone. He found his new roommate to be friendly. Smit was not impressed by Kershaw's stature, primarily because he was unaware of it. "I actually had no idea," Smit explained. "I didn't find out until almost two weeks in. I was like, "Holy shit." He's legit." At that point, Smit realized Kershaw operated on a different level. "I just showed up and played," Smit explained. Kershaw went through his extended stretching ritual before throwing. In between excursions, he studied opponents' primitive hitting charts. He seemed at ease clanging and pounding in the weight room. He never seemed to fatigue. "He was way above everybody else, way above me," Smit remarked.

The minor league system functioned as a thresher. There was precious little wheat and plenty of chaff. Almost all of the players who donned uniforms and declared themselves professionals would never play in the major leagues. In the majors, money distinguished between stars and scrubs. In the minors, where teams like the Dodgers paid all Gulf Coast League players roughly $300 per week, a caste structure emerged depending on the player's signing bonus. Kershaw stood on top of Vero Beach's pyramid in the summer of 2006. He had received the biggest bonus in Dodgers franchise history. Mattingly signed for $1 million. The prices decreased in subsequent rounds. Smit was selected 136 picks after Kershaw and received a $175,000 bonus. Trayvon Robinson, the tenth-round pick in 2005, signed for $50,000.

Then there were those like Dave Preziosi. He did not get picked after graduating from Boston College. Nearly twenty years after his job ended, he could remember his bonus to the last decimal point: "Nothing," he remarked. "Zero dollars." In a manner, signing with the Dodgers cost him $800 because he had been playing in Germany and had paid for his return flight. Preziosi belonged on the island of misfit toys. His fastball was somewhere in the 70s. He threw the sidearm. His delivery was, in a word, weird. "I had a really funky motion where I kicked my glove and brought my body momentum down to really get down low," according to him. His claim to fame is striking out Red Sox hitter David Ortiz with a 55-mph slider during an exhibition. "He had never seen something that slow," Preziosi recounted.

Preziosi was aware that his time had been borrowed. But for one summer, he could confuse young hitters in the Gulf Coast League. Preziosi compared his stats to those of the Golden Boy. "I would be like, 'You signed for $2.3 million, and I didn't sign for anything—and I have a better ERA than you,'" Preziosi laughed. Kershaw typically laughs it off. But one afternoon, after being pestered enough, Kershaw yelled, "At least I don't have to resort to kicking my glove to extend a baseball career that's clearly going nowhere!" Preziosi erupted with laughter. Kershaw apologized instantly. Preziosi stewed in the clubhouse later that summer, when he got high. His mood lifted when he noticed Kershaw laughing.

The players lived in a group of bungalows. When the Melsons arrived, driving from Amelia Island, they were surprised by the bare-bones arrangement. "Two beds, one bathroom," Smit recalled. "Pretty much like a Motel 6." The staff served three meals per day. There were games in the afternoon. At night, the men lounged around the facility. They held Xbox competitions for FIFA and Madden. Kershaw accompanied Mattingly whenever he drove to Taco Bell. They cashed their paychecks at the nearest Walmart. Sometimes they went bowling. A trip to the mall signified the pinnacle of exhilaration.

Kershaw stood out while blending in. Throughout the day, the talent blinded his teammates. In the evenings, however, "You would never realize that he was the one on the team who had just signed a massive contract," said Jason Schwab, a New Orleans outfielder. Kershaw did not brag about his fastball or bonus. He never swore. If he teased someone, he did it gently. Trayvon Robinson described Kershaw as a "sweet guy." If he noticed a roach, he would probably avoid stepping on it. "He would walk around it."

That goodwill did not extend to opposing lineups. "When he pitched," Schwab recounted, "you weren't going to have much to do, and it was going to end quickly." After one game, Mattingly called his father, who was then the Yankees' hitting coach. "Dad," Preston teased Don, "we've got a guy who can beat you guys right now." He was so talented that the other players wondered why he was on the field with them. Robinson observed Kershaw's first bullpen after his signing. "It was like, 'Nah, he ain't going to be here long,'" Robinson said. The catcher behind the plate felt the same way. Kenley Jansen, a huge backstop from the Caribbean island of Curaçao, thought, "This kid doesn't belong here."

Kershaw played in ten games that summer. He struck out 54 of 144 hitters he faced. He had a 1.95 ERA. "He looked like he didn't belong in that league," said Daniel Murphy, the New York Mets' recent draft pick. Kershaw even recorded a save by throwing to Jansen to finish out a postseason game. Some in the organization were unhappy by his relief appearance, questioning why the Dodgers would put his health at risk for a minor-league title. "I was pissed," White recalls. When the season concluded, the Dodgers assigned Kershaw to Arizona's instructional league. He shared a room with Mattingly in Peoria. The posting felt like a continuation of the Gulf Coast League: baseball during the day, FIFA and Madden at night. Again, Kershaw's presence perplexed his contemporaries. "I was like, 'Man, why is this guy here?'" Robinson recalls. "I'm here attempting to switch hits. What is Kershaw supposed to work on?"

The Dodgers gave Kershaw a mission that would haunt him for the rest of his career: learn a changeup. His two-pitch mix, fastball and curveball, was adequate against low-level competition. However, the Dodgers did not anticipate Kershaw to remain in the minors for long. He needed a third alternative. When properly performed, the changeup disrupts a hitter's timing. Dodgers officials believed that combining it with a heater like Kershaw's would be overwhelming.

Except that Kershaw couldn't throw it. At the very least, he couldn't throw it to a standard that he considered acceptable. The pitch necessitated variation in the movement of his wrist as he launched the baseball. He hurled it repeatedly. Still, the pitch stank. He informed team management that he wanted to scrap it and focus on the two pitches he had. Marty Reed, the organization's minor-league pitching coordinator, instructed him that one of the first two pitches Kershaw threw to each hitter must be a changeup.

The mandate did not instill trust in Kershaw. It only infuriated him. Following one game, Kershaw approached Reed and apologized. Kershaw was mortified that he had walked so many batters. Reed urged him not to worry; this was a learning experience. No, Kershaw insisted. He needed to improve.

Reed took Kershaw out to dinner one night and questioned him about his goals: "Who do you want to be?" What type of career do you want? Kershaw didn't address the Dodgers' legacy. He did not specify which players he hoped to mimic. He told Reed he hoped to make it to the major leagues. He wanted to provide for his mother. And he wanted to give his all to his craft.

When Kershaw returned to Texas after the season, he purchased a car. He hadn't possessed one before. His father had loaned him his Ford Explorer a few years ago. Clayton drove it for a long time without insurance until Chris took it back. Clayton now had his own money, and he knew exactly what he wanted. He spent $37,000 for a black Ford F-150 King Ranch pickup with a leather inside. "My dream car," he described it.

One day in February 2007, Kershaw pointed the truck south towards College Station. Clayton and Ellen had communicated via phone and email throughout the season. She pledged the Chi Omega sorority during her first month at university. When Kershaw came to visit, he felt out of place. "Where do you attend school?"Other kids inquired. "I don't go to school," Kershaw said without explanation. Ellen asked him to explain his occupation, lest her new acquaintances question why she was dating a burnout. He once informed one of her sorority sisters that he worked for Walmart. He slept on couches across the Texas A&M Greek community. He could usually only stay there for two nights before wanting to depart.

Nonetheless, they had reached an equilibrium. After a few months apart, Ellen realized she could handle the distance. "Everybody's under the impression, like, 'You're going to want to be single in college,'" she told me. "That wasn't me. I wasn't trying to be single and date around." So they made the most of their time together. For one themed party, they dressed as Clark and Ellen Griswold. On that February trip, they talked till early in the morning at her sorority house. They both admitted that they were not drinking. Kershaw slammed into some neighboring furniture before getting up early to go home.

Kershaw slept for only a few hours. He did not yet consume coffee. On the roadway, his eyes were closed.

"I fell asleep and hit those grooves on the side of the road," Kershaw explained. "It woke me up. And I went voom!"

The truck flipped twice. Kershaw emerged with just one scratch on his arm. He trembled at the thought of what may have transpired. His van included one of his forearm weights, a ten-pounder attached to a pole. "And it was just flopping around in my back seat," he remembered. "Could you imagine if that had…"

His dream automobile had been totaled. He never drove it again. But he was OK. The paramedics transported him to a hospital near campus. Ellen was conversing when her phone rang. When she saw her boyfriend's name, she refused the call. She assumed Kershaw was trying to pass the time while driving. He called again. And again. She eventually answered and dashed to see him.

Later that day, Kershaw contacted Logan White to explain the accident. He needed to shake off his near-death experience in order to prepare for his first full professional season. Even after more than a decade, when he had matured and become a parent, he struggled to put the accident in context.

"What did I get out of the experience? I don't know," Kershaw said. "Do not fall asleep while driving. I do not know. I honestly don't know. Just a miracle."

CHAPTER 5
DAWN OF DOMINANCE

*C*layton Kershaw was about to embark on one of the most devastating streaks by a starting pitcher in modern baseball. He threw his first slider during a game in Philadelphia on June 4, 2009. His ERA during his last twenty-one appearances that season was 2.03. Kershaw was approaching a time in which he was, as teammate Nathan Eovaldi put it, "untouchable." A generation of pitchers would study him, unable to recreate his repertoire. A generation of hitters would quake in his wake, unable to understand his attack. His time as a promising prospect was nearing an end. His reign as baseball's top pitcher was about to start.

In 2009, Kershaw played a supporting role to Manny Ramírez as the Dodgers' star. Ramírez was unpredictable, annoying, and unstoppable. After the Dodgers were eliminated in 2008, Bill Plaschke of the Los Angeles Times questioned Ramírez if he wanted to remain with the franchise. "We'll see," Ramírez answered. His free agency ruled the winter. Ramírez sat at home in Florida, waiting for the Dodgers to meet his price. Ramírez signed a two-year, $45 million contract and arrived at Camelback Ranch. He scared pitchers in April as if nothing was wrong.

Kershaw took the mound in Game 1 of the National League Championship Series. The Philadelphia Phillies were the reigning world champions, with a fearsome lineup and unwavering confidence. Ryan Howard, the imposing first baseman, had won the National League MVP in 2006. Jimmy Rollins, the irrepressible shortstop, received the same honor the following year. Chase Utley, the five-tool second baseman, was the standout of the group. Philadelphia wielded psychological power after defeating the Dodgers the year before. Wolf compared it to a horror film, saying the Dodgers played as if waiting for a monster to emerge from the closet.

They did not have to wait very long. Kershaw maintained a 1-0 lead until the fifth inning, when veteran outfielder Raúl Ibañez singled. Kershaw went on to unravel. He threw a wayward pitch and gave a walk. The visit of Rick Honeycutt had little effect. Kershaw gave up a three-run home run to Carlos Ruiz. The spiral only continued. Kershaw walked the opposition pitcher, Cole Hamels, after four pitches. Two more errant pitches followed. Utley walked. Howard hit a two-run double. Kershaw was unable to control the pace. He resisted the advice of many, including Honeycutt, Mike Borzello, and Glenn Dishman, to slow down the game. Kershaw attempted to overpower a lineup that he could not dominate. His fastball didn't bother them. He couldn't find his curveball. And his slider did not frighten the Phillies. "The early slider that he was throwing wasn't very good, to be honest with you," Utley told me later. "You could see the rotation fairly early." (Utley had a talent for spotting things; when he joined the Dodgers years later, he revealed a secret to his new teammates: In 2008 and 2009, the Phillies frequently knew what was coming because they swiped the Dodgers' signs from second base.)

Torre eventually intervened following Howard's double. Kershaw held a towel in the dugout and glanced at his cleats. He was too young to accept responsibility for the defeat; in the following day's Times, Plaschke chastised Torre for laissez-faire management. "Kershaw will probably be a No. 1 playoff starter for the next several years," Plaschke said. "But for now, he is still learning his craft, and he still needs to be saved from himself." Kershaw blamed himself for not slowing down and defusing the threat. "I'm trying to see all these bumps in the road as part of the process of becoming the man and pitcher I want to be," he wrote a few months later. The process sometimes be painful: "I sometimes wish the Lord were not quite so faithful to remind me, 'Clayton, you don't have it all figured out.'"

Kershaw never had a second chance to start against Philadelphia. After winning Game 2, the Dodgers were hammered in Game 3. Broxton blew a save against Philadelphia in the fourth game for the second time this postseason. "You got the impression that you could smell burned toast against the Phillies," Wolf told me. Kershaw, facing elimination, was refreshed and prepared. In the days before Game 5, he approached Torre in the weight room. Torre used an exercise bike to read the newspaper while wearing headphones. Kershaw stalked the room "like a caged animal," Wolf said. Torre looked up. Kershaw asked if he would start Game 5. "No," Torre replied. "You're out." The Dodgers chose Vicente Padilla. He allowed six runs. Kershaw allowed two more in relief. Another season concluded with opponents building a dogpile. "Those experiences," he claimed, "keep my competitive heart humble."

Ellen Melson wept inside her childhood bedroom one winter night, fatigued from riding roller coasters all afternoon with Kershaw at Six Flags. They were meant to have supper that night, but the details didn't matter. She was convinced that her lover was making a mistake.

Ellen had visited Kershaw in Los Angeles in 2009, the summer before her senior year at Texas A&M; Kershaw was still living with the Colemans downtown, but he was throwing well enough to see a future in the city. For the first time, the pair considered marriage. Ellen had her own life back in Texas, where she studied communications and participated in campus philanthropy. During the summer, she served as a missionary with AIDS orphans in Zambia. With graduation approaching, she wanted to be close to Kershaw. However, she did not want to uproot herself for someone who was not ready to commit.

Following the season, Ellen waited and hoped for a proposal. To her dismay, Kershaw kept disregarding the subject. Unbeknownst to Ellen, Clayton called her father and begged to meet with him so he could stammer a plea for her hand. Jim Melson found the nervousness amusing before giving his assent. Kershaw consulted Ellen's older sister, Ann, when planning the huge gesture. When he invited Ellen on that post-roller-coaster date a few days before Christmas, she missed the apparent cues: Clayton, the guy who despised pants, arrived in a new suit, his beard trimmed, in a white extended limousine. They drove through Highland Park, savoring the holiday lights, before dining downtown. Ellen was still unsure about the purpose of the evening when Clayton instructed the driver to stop at his apartment before leaving her off.

As Ellen approached the door, she noticed a glow in the windows: Christmas music, greenery, and lights. The floor was coated in snow made from dried ice. Upstairs, beneath the tree, sat one box. Ellen opened it and discovered a Santa Claus figurine holding her engagement ring. Ellen wept again, but this time she cried happy tears. They returned to the Melsons' house to find a party waiting for them. They discussed a wedding date. Of course, it would occur during the offseason.

In the spring of 2010, as the Dodgers reassembled at Camelback Ranch to begin another season, Kershaw asked Logan White for a favor. The draft was several months distant. Kershaw asked White to check out an old travel-ball teammate. "I didn't know who the heck Shawn Tolleson was," White said.

The majority of the other outstanding pitchers from Team USA and D-Bat had made it to the majors. Brett Anderson made 30 starts for Oakland in 2009. Tyson Ross made his debut for San Diego in the spring of 2010. Jordan Walden, the flamethrower who went from No. 1 in the country to the twelfth round, played for the Angels that summer. But Tolleson was struggling at Baylor. In college, while recovering from Tommy John surgery, he never regained the hellacious slider that made him Team USA's relieving ace. "They just assumed that I was going to just remember everything that got me to that level," he added. "And I didn't remember any of it." As a senior, he had a 5.17 ERA with a 2-7 record. He'd started applying to dental and medical schools.

On Kershaw's recommendation, White dispatched a scout to evaluate Tolleson. The report was skeptical. The Dodgers entered Tolleson into their draft database. And then White forgot about him. At least until the day of the draft, when White invited Kershaw to the conference room with the other scouts. "What about my pal Tolleson?" Kershaw inquired. "Where have you gotten him?" White admitted that Tolleson had faded from his memory. However, in the thirtieth round, the Dodgers took a gamble. Tolleson signed for $10,000 and was assigned to the team's rookie-ball affiliate in Ogden, Utah. A few years later, he made it to the majors. A couple of years later, he saved 35 games for a Texas Rangers team that made the playoffs. He damaged his back and then had a second Tommy John surgery, thus ending his career. Nonetheless, he earned almost $5 million more than he expected. "Who knows what my life would have turned out like?"Tolleson recalled."

Kershaw and Tolleson remained close over the years. They hung out during the winter and told each other stories about their children. Tolleson knew because White had informed him that Kershaw had launched his career. However, Tolleson never asked Kershaw about the draft. Kershaw never mentioned it.

Dodger Stadium deteriorated during McCourt's final years in office. In 2009, McCourt and his wife, Jamie, split, and the business nearly collapsed. McCourt had always run the Dodgers like a man outrunning his creditors. A culture of ass-covering pervaded the environment. Following the divorce, financing for players, personnel, and stadium upgrades dwindled. Dodger Stadium became a metaphor for ruin. The elevators crawled. There was only one batting cage in the stadium. The Dodgers shared a weight room with the visiting squad. Orlando Hudson, a four-time Gold Glove second baseman, was playing for Arizona when he first met Kershaw in the weight room. A year later, Hudson signed with Los Angeles. Kershaw compared Hudson to his former colleague, the maniacally motivated Roy Halladay, who won Cy Young Awards in Toronto and Philadelphia. Kershaw, who was barely over the drinking age, injected youthful energy into his rigorous routine. Kershaw was "always sweating," according to Hudson. "Like, 'Dude, what are you doing now?'I just completed running.' Two hours later: 'Dude, why are you sweating right now?'I just got out of the chilly tub.' Jeez, almighty! I really enjoyed that. That was not for show. "He did it every day."

Kershaw was learning how to maximize his time. His bullpen sessions got more efficient. Borzello described his big-league debut as "like a young stallion." Borzello warned Kershaw about the significance of commanding his pitches in that situation. He pushed Kershaw to locate a solid, low fastball, hammering the area of the zone where Kershaw would live. The sessions became neat, thirty-four pitch events, with the emphasis on repeating his delivery rather than increasing his velocity. He didn't dwell on shaky sessions or boast about perfect ones. He checked the box and proceeded with his day. "It didn't matter whether good, bad, or indifferent, he would leave it there," Honeycutt told me.

Honeycutt observed Kershaw was tilting as he pitched out of the stretch with runners on base. Kershaw clutched the baseball tightly when throwing a fastball, but his glove stretched as he searched for an off-speed grip. Honeycutt advised Kershaw to raise his hands and take a breather as he settled into the grip. The movement concealed his intentions while releasing tension in his shoulders. Kershaw no longer stood still, except for the unmistakable twitch in his glove. Over time, the maneuver became a signature. Kershaw stretched his hands higher and higher, until they were completely extended, pointing to the heavens as he exhaled.

Kershaw frequently received recommendations from coaches, bosses, or teammates. He dismissed the majority, but used the ones that made sense. "Early on, at that level, you'll try to do everything a coach tells you to do," said former Dodgers first-round draft pick Blake DeWitt. "And some guys just keep saying 'yes' and 'yes' and 'yes,' and they keep going down this trail that eventually leads them to forgetting who they are as a player." Kershaw," said DeWitt, "was hard-headed enough that he knew what made him great, and he was going to stick with it, whether somebody wanted him to be like that or not."

Torre rewarded Kershaw with trust. Kershaw threw 100 pitches in sixteen of his thirty starts in 2009. A year later, he did it twenty-seven times. He analyzed Honeycutt's charts for game plans. Kershaw wanted basic but important information: which hitters were aggressive early in the count? Where were the sweet spots? Where were the holes? He memorized the information before the games. Success led to conviction, which led to even greater success and conviction. "He fully believed," Brad Ausmus told me afterwards, "when he was standing on the mound that he was going to get you out, no matter who you were."

On July 20, 2010, Kershaw faced off for the first time with the National League West's top pitcher. The crown would soon belong to no one other than Kershaw, but Tim Lincecum had earned it. As Kershaw struggled through his first two seasons in the majors, Lincecum, a five-foot-eleven, 170-pound dynamo taken at No. 10 in the 2006 draft, captivated with his whirling-dervish delivery, a "engineering marvel," in the words of Sports Illustrated's Tom Verducci, who "generates outrageous rotational power—the key element to velocity—only because his legs, hips, and torso work in such harmony."

The synergy resulted in successive National League Cy Young Awards in 2008 and 2009. It also caused significant commotion in the Dodgers' executive office. "I remember Ned asking, 'How'd you guys pass on Lincecum?'" Dodgers scout Tim Hallgren remembered. They had their reasons. When Roy Smith and Logan White discussed Lincecum before the draft, they concluded that he provided a great return but an enormous risk. Lincecum's delivery was remarkable because of his right arm's incredible speed, which no pitcher could maintain for long. "I remember thinking, if he loses just a little bit of arm speed, he's screwed, at that size," Smith told me. In his first two seasons, Lincecum's fastball averaged 94 mph. He lost considerable velocity in 2009. He lost significantly more in 2010. The lightning was flashing out of his small body.

On that July night, when Kershaw and Lincecum took the mound for the first time, the matchup was still considered premier. Kershaw hit Giants outfielder Andrés Torres on the left hand with a 91.3-mph fastball in his first at-bat. There was history between the two parties. The Dodgers and Giants have always had a history together. Padilla had already shattered Giants outfielder Aaron Rowand's jaw with a pitch a few months before. After Kershaw clipped Torres, Lincecum threw three inside pitches toward Kemp. The third ultimately hit Kemp in the back.

When the officials threatened both benches with ejection, Dodgers bench coach Bob Schaefer yelled in outrage. He wasn't the only person angry in the dugout. Even when he wasn't pitching, Kershaw stuck out on the fence, rooting for his team. "That guy is Mr. Dodger," former teammate Jamey Wright remarked. To witness his teammates being tormented on a day when he had control of the baseball triggered the same protective feelings that previously had him throwing haymakers in a rookie football scrum.

Kershaw contacted Torre and Schaefer.

"Joe," Kershaw continued, "I'm getting somebody."

Torre described retaliation as unwise. The Dodgers might handle this in the future. They'd see the Giants again. Torre walked away to get a cup of water after dispensing wisdom. Kershaw remained unaffected.

"Schaef," he informed the bench coach, "I'm getting somebody."

Schaefer used the same spiel. An inning later, San Francisco reliever Denny Bautista brushed off Russell Martin. Martin spun out of the batter's box. The umpire dismissed Schaefer after he turned "ballistic." Schaefer spotted Kershaw while walking through the dugout. "I'll see you in a little while," Kershaw said.

Kershaw hit Rowand in the hip with his first pitch of the seventh inning. The umpire directed Kershaw to the showers. There were no histrionics or staged protests. The audience gave him a standing ovation. "To me," Schaefer said, "he's been a special guy ever since." Schaefer coached in the major leagues for nearly fifteen years. He proposed a theory regarding the intersection of talent and desire. "Some players," he observed, "are afraid to be good." They were concerned about the spotlight. They grappled with expectations. They shied away from the labor. Clayton Kershaw, he concluded, was not like that.

"He had the goal of being the best in the game," Schaefer said. "Many people do this in their own minds, but they also recognize their own limitations. And Kershaw refused to let any constraints stand in his way."

On December 4, 2010, seven years, nine months, and fifteen days after approaching a girl with brown hair in Highland Park High's hallways, Kershaw stood before the altar of Highland Park Presbyterian Church. The same woman was walking toward him.

Ellen continued to make him laugh all those years later, even after family trips with the Melsons and innumerable conversations and emails connecting his baseball world with her college life. She exuded optimism and pushed him beyond his comfort zone. "The best word to describe Ellen is just joyful," Kershaw added. "She's so joyful, positive, and enthusiastic." In Kershaw, Ellen discovered stability. "I want to see the world through rose-colored glasses," Ellen stated. "Part of it is because I know I have Clayton's security, who will check all the boxes, ensure that we're in good standing, and assess all the threats. I only get to look at the rewards." They complimented one another. "If there were two of us with heads in the clouds, it wouldn't work," Ellen told me.

The bride wore a strapless silk taffeta gown. In his black tuxedo, the groom donned a white tie and a daffy smile. Ellen's sister, Ann, served as the matron of honor. Josh Meredith led a group of groomsmen that comprised several Highland Park pals, Tolleson, and Ellen's two brothers. Baseball players in attendance included James McDonald, Preston Mattingly, and Paul Coleman. Following the ceremony, the group headed to Royal Oaks Country Club for the reception. The bar offered Lasorda Family Wines. The choir sings Christmas carols. The couple's first dance departed from tradition. A few days before the wedding, they were at a loss. A traditional ballad would not have fit their atmosphere; they would have felt out of place listening to "Wonderful Tonight." Ellen recalled her early enthusiasm. "I think we should choreograph a dance," she informed him. So, on the day of his wedding, Kershaw changed into sneakers and strutted through Ellen's routine for Usher's "DJ Got Us Fallin' in Love. I don't know how I convinced him to do it, but he did it," Ellen said.

They lied about their age on their honeymoon. They searched for "all-inclusive resorts in Mexico" and ended up in Playa Mujeres. They sipped fruity beverages by the pool while Kershaw threw baseballs at pillows to keep his arm fresh. A few weeks later,

Clayton traveled to Zambia for the first time with Ellen. Ellen noticed Kershaw's anxiousness in the months before the trip. He wasn't scared about the mission or the possibility of contracting malaria. He didn't want to disrupt his throwing program. He packed a cushioned mat on the plane. Once in the nation, he hired a welder to create a frame for the pad.

When they arrived in the capital, Lusaka, they ran across some of the youngsters Ellen recognized from prior travels. A mob of children assembled. Some stared at Kershaw; Ellen wondered if they'd ever seen a white guy so tall. She squeezed her husband's hand. "This is incredible," he told her. The trip strengthened his faith and helped him grasp Ellen's passion for the country. He was stirred while listening to the Zambians sing at mass. "Ellen had always told me that she thought worship in Zambia was a picture of what worship in heaven would look like," he wrote. "At that moment, I knew what she was talking about."

Kershaw maintained his fitness routine. He ran along dusty roads. He peppered the mat with pitches. Another person on the tour had played high school baseball, so Kershaw assigned him to play catch. The two trips prepared Ellen for what her future vacations would entail.

"I wish that sixteen years ago I had just learned to catch him," Ellen told me. "Because it would make our traveling so much easier if I could just do that."

In the winter, when he wasn't throwing to pillows, homemade targets, or gym class heroes, Kershaw solicited pitchers to join him at Highland Park High's indoor facility. The gathering ranged from high school friends to major league starters. Brandon McCarthy, a Texas Rangers right-hander, joined the team one offseason. He learned personally why Kershaw terrorized hitters. Kershaw connected when he established a target. McCarthy simply could not track the ball's arrival. "I remember that popping out right away, like, 'Oh, that's why you can't really hit this. "You can't pick it up," McCarthy recalled.

McCarthy stood by Will Skelton, Kershaw's former Highland Park teammate who was nearing the end of his career at Sam Houston State. Skelton observed that Kershaw's velocity was deceptive. His average fastball was 93 mph, but the ball appeared to be traveling quicker. "I would love for someone to do an analysis of how many more rotations his ball does at sixty feet than mine," he told McCarthy.

In the coming years, the fleet of aeronautical engineers, spreadsheet gurus, and analytically observant Moneyball acolytes that dominated baseball front offices would be able to provide an answer: Kershaw's over-the-top delivery generated enormous volumes of backspin. The simplest way to describe this phenomenon is to consider an airplane. When a plane lifts off, the airfoil generates upward thrust beneath its wings. Backspin in baseball operates in the same way. The concept of a "rising fastball" is a fiction. No human can generate that much force. However, a pitcher like Kershaw may be able to generate enough backspin to battle gravity for an extended period of time. His fastball fell later than others, causing perceptual uncertainty for hitters. "His fastball was such a difficult pitch to hit in his prime," said Joey Votto, the Cincinnati Reds' first baseman. The heater did not follow the predicted path. "God dang, dude," said veteran outfielder Reed Johnson, who specialized in facing left-handed pitchers. "It just gets on you more than other guys."

"He had one of those fastballs that nobody really knew how to quantify," said Matt Carpenter, Kershaw's rival with the St. Louis Cardinals. "You just knew it was way harder than what [the velocity] said."

On November 17, 2011, the Dodgers held a coronation for Clayton

Kershaw. His singular brilliance illuminated a year of collective failure and institutional disgrace. After the first game of the season, two Dodgers supporters assaulted Bryan Stow, a San Francisco Giants fan, in an ill-lit Dodger Stadium parking lot. Stow spent months in a medically induced coma; his plight served as a "sobering reminder," as the New York Times put it, that the ballpark "no longer seems to fit its former image, and that many fans have become uneasy going there." The Los Angeles Times reported in April that McCourt required a $30 million loan to make payroll. A few days later, citing "deep concerns regarding the Dodgers' finances and operations," commissioner Bud Selig said Major League Baseball would take over the organization. Later that summer, the franchise went bankrupt.

A spate of injuries destroyed a roster that had been weakened by McCourt's austerity measures. Logan White's fleet of prospects ran aground. Russell Martin left through free agency. Jonathan Broxton never recovered from his October beating by Philadelphia. Chad Billingsley recorded the worst ERA of his career. There was no new wave coming up behind them. McCourt had depleted the money for overseas free agents, while White had placed a string of losing first-round wagers on high school players such as Chris Withrow, Ethan Martin, and Zach Lee.

The bleakness allowed the franchise to enjoy its individual accomplishments, namely Kershaw and Kemp. Kemp rebounded off a difficult 2010 season in which he clashed with Joe Torre's coaching staff. He thrived after Don Mattingly became manager in 2011. Kemp stole 40 bases while leading the National League with 39 home runs and 126 RBI. Nonetheless, he finished second to Milwaukee Brewers slugger Ryan Braun in the National League MVP voting. The disappointment got worse when ESPN revealed that Braun had tested positive for a performance-enhancing drug earlier that season. Despite finishing second, Kemp signed an eight-year, $160 million contract.

Aside from Kemp and Kershaw's domination, the Dodgers never gained traction in 2011. In early September, Kershaw faced Lincecum for the fourth time that year. The Dodgers won each game by a single run. Lincecum would finish sixth in the Cy Young voting for his final top season. By then, Kershaw had surpassed him. On that September afternoon in San Francisco, as Kershaw was blanking the Giants, Josh Lindblom sat next to Ellis on the bench. At the time, baseball clubhouses were rife with debate over Christopher Nolan's new film about the ravages of dreams and memory. "How much money," Lindblom asked Ellis, "would it take to approach Clayton and ask him what he thought of the ending of Inception?"

Unfazed by queries about Leonardo DiCaprio's spinning top, Kershaw struck out nine in eight innings of one-run ball. The game helped him win the pitcher's triple crown, as he led the National League in wins (21), ERA (2.28), and strikeouts (248). He easily won his first National League Cy Young Award, with twenty-seven of thirty-two first-place votes from the Baseball Writers' Association of America, beating out Philadelphia's Roy Halladay and Cliff Lee. Kershaw, at twenty-two, became the youngest pitcher to win the award since twenty-year-old Met Dwight Gooden stunned New York in 1985.

CHAPTER 6
WEIGHT OF THE GAME

*O*n April 28, 2013, Kershaw drove alone to Dodger Stadium to face the Milwaukee Brewers. After he went to the ballpark, Ellen received a call from Chris Kershaw's wife. Chris had died. Ellen pondered how to inform Clayton. She was worried that he might receive the news from someone other than her.

A. J. Ellis had the day off and watched from the bench as Kershaw struck out twelve in eight shutout innings. A staffer grabbed Ellis midway through the game; Ellen needed to speak with him outside the clubhouse. Ellis rushed out of the dugout. Ellen asked Ellis to get Kershaw's phone. She didn't want him to stumble upon texts regarding Chris.

Ellen served as a buffer between Kershaw and his father's relatives. Her connection with Chris was less tense. "It was just too much for Clayton," Ellen explained. "There was just part of Clayton, like, I don't know, not knowing what that relationship was supposed to look like, and so kind of wanting to keep it at a distance." She waited in the depths of Dodger Stadium, in a tunnel leading to the clubhouse, until Kershaw departed the game. He came down a set of steps and noticed her. She told him. They packed his belongings and exited the ballpark. "For some reason, it's, like, cloudy to me, the whole memory of it all," Kershaw told me afterwards.

Kershaw returned to Dallas for the funeral. He asked a Highland Park student to catch his bullpen. He rejoined the squad in time for his next start in San Francisco. He refused to discuss his previous travels. When Clayton Kershaw spoke about Chris Kershaw with those outside his personal circle, he focused on the positive memories from the years before the divorce. He imagined the father playing hoops with his son, not the broken man in the hospital bed. "We could always just do that," Kershaw said. "I used to play catch a lot, but I started throwing too hard. He accomplished all of that. As a dad should. Clayton learnt about parenting from Chris, and I am grateful for that. He knew the type of father he wanted to be.

Following the burial, Kershaw returned to a feuding team. He pitched seven innings of one-run ball against the Giants, but the Dodgers lost, continuing their eight-game losing streak. Very little had gone well for the large spenders. Ramírez suffered a torn thumb ligament during the World Baseball Classic. Greinke fractured his left collarbone during his second start when San Diego Padres outfielder Carlos Quentin attacked the mound after Greinke plunked him. A week later, Chad Billingsley had pain in his right elbow, which foreshadowed his impending Tommy John surgery. Matt Kemp, one of the few surviving homegrown players drafted by Logan White, struggled as he returned from offseason shoulder surgery; Kemp would never again compete for MVP. All the injuries and losses sparked potshots. "When the Titanic sank," Dylan Hernández wrote in the Times that April. "There was a Guggenheim on board."

Don Mattingly, the man in charge of keeping this ocean liner afloat, was unsure whether this was his final season as manager of the team. Mattingly was one of the best players of his time, a former MVP who many thought belonged in the Hall of Fame. His reputation was impeccable. "He's cloaked in kindness, and he's cloaked in humility," explained Trey Hillman, Mattingly's bench coach from 2011 to 2013. Mattingly united with his union compatriots throughout the 1980s collusion scandals and against the Yankees' outmoded grooming procedures. He had the misfortune of playing in the Bronx during a rare down phase. After retiring in 1995 due to back difficulties and a desire to nurture his children, the Yankees won four titles in five seasons. Mattingly raised his children, including Kershaw's friend

Preston, before returning to the game. Mattingly left a lasting impression on players of a specific age. "I grew up idolizing Don Mattingly," retired infielder Jamey Carroll said. Mattingly recognized how difficult baseball might be, but he never boasted about his personal accomplishments. "He just had zero ego," Casey Blake recalled.

Mattingly created a welcoming environment. In the spring of 2012, the team employed a mop-topped guy named John Pratt as video coordinator. Pratt had recently graduated from Emerson College in Boston, where he studied broadcast journalism. The clubhouse intimidated him. Mattingly paid daily visits to the video room. "He's the nicest man in the world," Pratt explained. Mattingly inquired about Pratt's family and his childhood. He treated him as one of the guys, mocking him for his oddities. "I made the mistake one time of telling him that I didn't like the shampoo in the Ritz-Carlton," Pratt told me. "And it gave him years of fodder."

Mattingly endured McCourt's twilight years, when the payroll was reduced and hope faded, only to find himself out on a limb in 2013. Mattingly lacked a long-term contract and confidence that the Dodgers wanted him around. He was annoyed by his status as a lame duck. Colletti had hired him, but Mattingly wondered if Kasten and the new staff trusted him. Mattingly remained optimistic as injuries devastated the roster. He remained calm in the face of rumors concerning his job position. And he juggled his stars' egos the entire time. All he wanted was the approval of a contract renewal.

In June, Kershaw joined the grumpy club. Talks halted after he rejected the $300 million deal. Later that summer, Kasten said, Close restarted conversations about the original seven-year framework. The negotiations came to a halt after Fox Sports' Ken Rosenthal claimed that the two parties were making progress. The story bothered Kershaw. He accused the Dodgers of breaking a mutual agreement not to discuss the trade publicly. The discussions proceeded; money tends to outweigh chivalry. They were on the verge of signing a $210 million contract when they began squabbling over how to insure it. Kasten and Smart engaged in yelling matches.

Kershaw's performance was unaffected by the uncertainty of the discussions or his future. That August, he made his third consecutive All-Star Game appearance. He lived on a five-day cycle. The day following his start, he lifted, ran, and played catch. On the second day, he completed his thirty-four pitch bullpen session. On the third day, he lifted and threw long tosses. On the fourth day, he mounted the bullpen mound to apply the visualization skills he had learned from Derek Lowe. On the sixth day, he ate a turkey sandwich and threw the baseball against the clubhouse walls before dominating on the field. The work he completed on the first four days enabled him to overcome the nervousness that took over his mind on the fifth day. He required the cycle because if he ignored it "and things didn't go well, there's just that feeling of, like, You really screwed this one up," he remembered. "The consistency and routine helps the mind."

It also gave Kershaw an unstable appearance to those who were unfamiliar with him. Michael Young, a seven-time All-Star third baseman for the Texas Rangers, lifted with Kershaw this winter. Colletti signed Young at the end of August 2013 to strengthen his bench. Young met with the team at Coors Field in Colorado on the day Kershaw was scheduled to start. When Young entered the clubhouse, he noticed his offseason training buddy. "Hey, 22! You suck!"Young said. Kershaw gave a half-smile and went away. Oh shit, Young thought. Young left his things in his locker and proceeded to the training room. Ellis was there. "First time playing with Kersh, right?"Ellis said.

By the time Young arrived, the Dodgers had clinched first place in the National League West. The team was in last place on June 3 when Colletti promoted Puig, a twenty-two-year-old signed to a $42 million contract following a brief audition with Logan White a year prior. Puig stood six feet two and weighed 240 pounds, straddling the line between arrogance and recklessness. He broke team rules about tardiness and got little discipline; some Dodgers believed Puig was sheltered by the new ownership group. But he could play, and the Dodgers were on a roll. "Winning does a lot," Kershaw remarked following one of his starts that summer. "It sets aside many differences, as well as bad blood. González's consistency, Ramírez's return, and Puig's arrival boosted the offense. Puig batted.319 with a.925 OPS that season. His electricity on the bases, as well as the rocket launcher he referred to as his right arm, energized Dodger Stadium. Following his promotion, the squad finished 69-38, winning the West by eleven games.

Kershaw was happy with the turnaround. He didn't want to miss any future October. On the four days he did not play, he took the top step of the Dodgers' dugout. He was "the biggest cheerleader ever," according to Skip Schumaker. "He's either eating, in uniform watching the game, or in a pile of his own sweat," Young told me. Kershaw climbed over the railing at Chase Field in Arizona on September 19 to celebrate the team's division championship. After the players sprayed champagne and domestic beer, Kershaw and the others went to the indoor pool beyond the right-field fence. Kershaw splashed and smiled with his teammates. Then he climbed out and dried himself off. His timetable called for visualizing the next day. He had more beginnings to make.

On October 3, the Dodgers, who had 92 wins, returned to the postseason for the first time since 2009, taking on the 96-win Atlanta Braves in the National League Division Series. Kershaw's most recent postseason appearance was 1,449 days ago. He was no longer a gifted youth full of potential but lacked elegance. In a few weeks, he would win his second Cy Young Award, placing first on twenty-nine of thirty ballots, following a season in which he had the sport's lowest ERA (1.83) and led the National League with 232 strikeouts. At the age of 25, he was baseball's top pitcher and the most essential player on one of the most costly squads ever built.

Despite some brave early at-bats by the Braves, Kershaw struck out 12 and held Atlanta to one run. His teammates built him a nice cushion. In the sixth inning, Hanley Ramírez's RBI double off Jordan Walden, Atlanta's relief pitcher, increased the advantage to five runs. Kershaw remained around for seven innings. He threw 124 pitches, his second highest total of the season. Kershaw pleaded for more after winning 6-1. "He was barking right after the game that he was ready for Game 4," Mattingly explained a few days later. "We're like, 'No, no, no, no, no.'"

In the early 1970s, the Dodgers pioneered the five-man rotation, which became the acknowledged standard and established the cycle that Kershaw would follow decades later. Starting pitchers became accustomed to taking the ball after four days off. The post-start lactic acid buildup in the arm required several days to dissipate. "When you pitch, your shoulder and elbow bleed," former manager Buck Showalter said. "And then you have to flush that out." In times of desperation, typically in October, teams urged their best pitchers to pitch more frequently. Curt Schilling made three starts for the Arizona Diamondbacks in the 2001 World Series, two of which were on short rest. CC Sabathia made two starts on short rest during the New York Yankees' 2009 championship season. In 2011, St. Louis Cardinals mainstay Chris Carpenter pitched Game 7 of the World Series on short rest. But they were the success stories; Greg Maddux was smoked in 2001. Kevin Brown had only four outs in 2004. Chien-Ming Wang pitched one inning in 2005.

The technique had mostly fallen out of favor. Matt Cain and Madison Bumgarner were given frequent rest while leading San Francisco to World Series victories in 2010 and 2012. The Phillies did not utilize Roy Halladay, Cliff Lee, or Cole Hamels on short rest in 2011. In

Detroit, Max Scherzer was willing to work as a reliever in postseason games between starts, but Justin Verlander stuck to his regular schedule. Zack Greinke made his postseason debut as a Milwaukee Brewer in the fall of 2011, allowing four runs in five innings on short rest after pitching in the final game of the regular season. He made twenty additional postseason appearances in the 2010s. Nobody was on short rest.

As Mattingly and Honeycutt planned the Dodgers' pitching schedule in 2013, they knew they could put Greinke behind Kershaw. Greinke had recovered from a shattered collarbone and finished with a 2.63 ERA. Hyun-Jin Ryu, the third starter, with a 3.0 ERA. However, the fourth starter posed a dilemma. Ricky Nolasco had given up 22 runs in 25.2 September innings. Mattingly informed reporters that Nolasco would start Game 4. However, in the weeks preceding up to the postseason, the Dodgers discussed utilizing Kershaw. "You never liked it, but we didn't have many options," Honeycutt recounted. "He was our best pitcher."

After losing Game 2, the Dodgers returned to Los Angeles. Kershaw, Ellis, and Pratt went to West Hollywood for pizza the day before Game 3. They had a couple pies and drinks before going to the Comedy Store. Ellis teased Kershaw about how these indulgences could disrupt his regimen. Kershaw responded that after three days of recuperation, he didn't know what the routine was. He was improvising by lifting less sets on the first day. He cut his bullpen session short on the second day. "I basically just skipped day three," he recounted, instead focusing on his fourth day visualization.

After the Dodgers won Game 3, Mattingly summoned Kershaw to his office. Kershaw listened as Colletti, Mattingly, and Honeycutt reminded him there was no need for fake swagger. "I think about this all winter long," Kershaw told them. Everything he accomplished, every day of his five-day cycle, every rep on the squat rack, every sprint in the outfield, led him to this point. He didn't care that he hadn't yet signed a long-term contract. He wanted the ball. Kershaw was grinning as he exited the office. Hillman told Mattingly that Kershaw looked "like a kid on Halloween who stole the biggest bag of candy you could ever see."

The Braves put up a fight. In the fourth inning, González made a throwing error, allowing a two-run rally. Kershaw held on for six innings, throwing 91 pitches and keeping the game tied. Puig doubled in the eighth inning, as Braves All-Star closer Craig Kimbrel watched from the bullpen, and infielder Juan Uribe homered to win the game. The Dodgers advanced to the National League Championship Series, where they would face the St. Louis Cardinals. Sandy Koufax, who is about to turn seventy-eight, wore goggles to protect himself from champagne spray during the noisy celebration. Koufax placed his arms around Kershaw's shoulders, expressing his respect. Kershaw considered Koufax neither a mentor nor a deity. He was a friend. "He's just a good human being," Koufax stated. They spoke on the phone and ate dinner whenever they could. They shared more than just an arsenal. Koufax had given up his left arm in quest of glory. Kershaw, he felt, had the same spirit. "The one thing that I appreciate about him a lot is, you never really have your best stuff," Koufax told me. "And when you figure out how to win when you don't have your best stuff, that's special."

The Cardinals won 97 games in 2013, more than any other team in the National League, keeping the baseball world on its axis. The Cardinals had reached the postseason ten times in the twenty-first century, winning the National League pennant four times and the World Series twice. The franchise maintained regional predominance in the Midwest, as represented by flagship station KMOX, "The Voice of St. Louis," which carried games in forty-four states. The fans promoted themselves as "The Best Fans in Baseball." The team hadn't missed a beat since organizational Mahatma Tony La Russa retired and three-time National League MVP Albert Pujols left after winning the 2011 World Series. "We believed in each other," Cardinals outfielder Jon Jay remarked. "We never quit."

Kershaw returned to his routine. Mattingly scheduled him for Game 2 at Busch Stadium. However, the series shifted before he took the mound—and even before Greinke took the mound in Game One. Cardinals pitcher Joe Kelly grew up in Corona, California, and ate his fair share of scraps. At a high school tryout camp, he decided to wow a group of scouts by heaving a baseball from the outfield to the third floor of a nearby building. Kelly, bespectacled and baby-faced, has incredible speed. He just wasn't sure where the baseball was heading. Kelly delivered a 95-mph two-seam sinker on his ninth delivery in the first game. The pitch hit Hanley Ramírez's rib cage instead of catcher Yadier Molina's glove, which was fortunate for the Cardinals.

In 2013, Ramírez played only 86 games due to injury after earning the National League batting title a couple years earlier. He was frail, yet important. Ramírez led the Dodgers to a 3-2 defeat after thirteen innings, with only one hit in 10 opportunities with runners in scoring position. The following day, Ramírez was unable to swing a bat due to soreness, forcing Mattingly to assemble a lineup without him or outfielder Andre Ethier, who had hurriedly recovered from shin splints in September. In Wacha's opinion, the prospect of matching Kershaw was more important than smothering the Dodgers lineup. "I remember thinking I couldn't give up anything, because he's not going to give up anything," according to him.

Kershaw lived up to his billing. After six innings, he had struck out five and held St. Louis to two hits. The Cardinals scored a run in the fifth when leadoff batter David Freese doubled, advanced to third after Ellis failed to grasp a fastball that skipped behind him for a passed ball, and scored on Jay's sacrifice fly. Kershaw had only thrown 72 pitches when his turn in the batting order came up in the sixth. Mattingly did not want to give up one of his last seven outs.

The hitters blamed themselves for squandering Kershaw's effort in a 1-0 loss that gave the Cardinals a two-game lead.

Despite a lack of offense, the Dodgers won two out of three games to extend the series. Ramírez batted .133. Puig struck out in ten of his twenty-two at bats. Ethier batted .150. Kemp had been sidelined in September because he needed ankle surgery. For all the money invested by Guggenheim, for all the hoopla produced around "The Best Team Money Can Buy," for all the instability the team endured during the summer, when the series came to St. Louis for Game 6, everything depended on Clayton Kershaw's left arm.

Kershaw was once again partnered against Wacha. "I probably really didn't know what I was doing out there, and the magnitude," Wacha laughed. Kershaw did. He leaned into his October look, growing his beard into an awkward chinstrap and letting his hair fall to his shoulders. He had pitched a career-high 236 innings during the regular season and another 19 in the postseason. He had trained all winter, prepared all spring, and worked hard all summer to achieve this mountain. He felt he was prepared.

In the second inning, Kershaw allowed a single and then spiked a pair of curveballs for wild pitches. He did not have a strong feel for the curve. The Cardinals were not going to tremble before him. The second point was cemented in a dramatic manner when second baseman Matt Carpenter walked up to the plate in the third. After selecting Carpenter in the thirteenth round of the 2009 draft, the Cardinals awarded him a meager $1,000 bonus. He had no leverage. He had already attended college for five years. The money was well spent. Carpenter advanced to the majors in his third professional season. He became a regular in 2012. He made his first All-Star squad in 2013. Carpenter appeared to have been selected from a casting call for La Russa. He avoided wearing batting gloves. He talked in a gentle, South Texas drawl. He saw more pitches than anybody else on his club. He exemplified the Cardinals' mindset, ruining good pitches while smacking bad ones. "If there was ever going to be a team that could combat what Clayton did, I think it would have been us," Carpenter told me. "We took pride in having those long, grinding at-bats, and making him work, making him earn it."

Kershaw used fastballs to overwhelm Carpenter in the first inning. Carpenter took a different tactic to their second confrontation. His goal was to avoid striking out. Carpenter held the bat on his shoulder while Kershaw missed inside with a first-pitch slider. He swung on the following seven deliveries. Carpenter fouled off one fastball, another, and a third. Carpenter fouled off Kershaw's curveball down the first base line. Carpenter battled off Kershaw's slider down the third base line. The sixth foul ball energized the fans. The seventh person was greeted by a soft roar. Carpenter felt like a tennis player defending against a devastating serve. He reasoned that as long as he could communicate, he would be alive. The tenth pitch was a ball within. It evened the score at 2-2. Carpenter received further acclaim when he diverted the tenth pitch, another fastball, into the fans. Kershaw composed himself and threw a slider. The ball was aimed at the glove-side portion of the plate, as it was with the majority of his pitches. Carpenter hit it to right field for a double. Left-handed hitters like Carpenter batted.165 against Kershaw during the regular season; when Kershaw threw two strikes, lefties batted.136. However, this was not the regular season.

A deluge ensued. Carlos Beltrán singled off the glove of second baseman Mark Ellis. Puig's ill-timed throw allowed Beltrán to reach second. After Kershaw struck out outfielder Matt Holliday, Molina singled up the middle to score Beltrán. Freese cut a hit just beneath Kershaw's glove. Kershaw yelled at the umpire when a 3-2 fastball to first baseman Matt Adams was ruled a ball. Kershaw attempted to remain composed, but outfielder Shane Robinson hit a two-run single. In total, the Cardinals scored four runs off four groundball singles, a close call on a full-count fastball, and Carpenter's stubbornness to yield. Kershaw lasted until the fifth inning, but when the first three Cardinals reached base—two singles, another terrible throw by Puig, and a double by Adams—Mattingly stepped in.

Kershaw turned over the baseball without protest. He took off his glove and examined his feet as he went to the dugout. Cardinals supporters hooted and swirled white towels all around him. The lineup only mustered two hits against Wacha in the 9-0 loss, but no one cared. Kershaw exploded in the biggest game of his career. The result left the team "shell-shocked," A. J. Ellis stated subsequently. "I don't have an answer," Kershaw replied. "I just wasn't good enough."

In a season of high expectations and competing egos, Kershaw had been the team's shining light. So he bore the brunt of the final defeat. He saw little solace in how the Dodgers recovered from early season struggles or how close the team had come to ending its title drought.

"What does it matter?" he stated. "Whether you make the playoffs or finish last, if you don't win the World Series, it makes little difference. What's the purpose if you don't win?"

Game 7," Kenley Jansen recalled, "nobody would have talked about it." In October, other Dodgers reasoned, Kershaw bore a heavier burden than any of his peers—pitching on short rest, in relief, and returning from injury. "Shit that no one's ever done, and that no one else would even be asked to do," Alex Wood said. "Consider any great pitchers heading to the Hall right now. Do you see any of those guys doing that?" His friend Will Skelton once computed Kershaw's playoff ERA without taking into account the runners other relievers allowed to score. "It's a particular sore spot for me," Skelton explained. Ellen considered utilizing social media to defend her husband, but ultimately decided against it. It would only make matters worse.

His phone was filled with messages from friends, enemies, teammates, people who competed with him, and those who respected him. Former Dodger Josh Lindblom frequently contacted Kershaw following his postseason defeats. The two men remained close even after Lindblom's work led him to Philadelphia, Oakland, and eventually Korea. "I don't think you can ever tell how much it hurt him, because he would never show it," she recounted. "But as you get to know him, you just know how much he cares."

Despite his anguish, Kershaw did not remain inactive. On his first day back in Texas, he led a six-hour camp in West Dallas for 400 children. Two weeks after Game 7, he began lifting. A month after Game 7, on his seventh wedding anniversary, he went to Los Angeles to sign two-way Japanese star Shohei Ohtani. "If we get this guy," he told Ellen, "it'll be worth it." (The Dodgers did not get that guy; "Just a gigantic waste of time," he said after Ohtani signed with the Los Angeles Angels.) Six weeks after Game 7, Kershaw picked up a baseball again.

As part of the exercises, Kershaw welcomed a new pitcher. "After the 2017 season, how it shook out, myself and my family, we were disappointed," Yu Darvish said in an interview. "During that difficult time, he reached out and invited me to play catch with him." Being a Dodger had energized Darvish; prior to the move, he had considered retiring. The World Series left him sad. Darvish felt the same sadness Kershaw did. Darvish had entered free agency, therefore they were no longer colleagues. Darvish was encouraged when Kershaw extended his hand. "He's very kind, in the sense that he considers other people," Darvish recalled.

Kershaw encouraged Darvish to return to the Dodgers. Darvish was concerned about how fans might respond to him. He feared his children would be harassed at school. When Farhan Zaidi came to Dallas to meet with Darvish, Kershaw joined him. Zaidi committed "probably one of the worst functional short-circuits of my life" while eating sushi, scooping wasabi with his fingers and absentmindedly scratching his face. "I've rarely felt that kind of pain in my life," Zaidi said. Both pitchers cackled as Zaidi staggered against tables on his way to the washroom. The pain was for naught: Darvish inked a six-year, $126 million contract with the Cubs, who paid more than the Dodgers.

That winter, Kershaw received another Dodger at Highland Park. Walker Buehler made his debut in September but watched the World Series from the stands. Team officials predicted Buehler will be ready in 2018. They questioned if Kershaw could be his mentor. The two formed an odd relationship. Buehler exuded confidence, which may be off-putting. Despite his young appearance, wiry stature, and lack of major-league experience, he spewed a lot of nonsense. And he cursed like the Kentucky horsemen he grew up with. A major chunk of his words were variations of the word "fuck"; it's difficult to imagine how much money he would have donated to Ellen's swear jar.

Grumpiness pervaded the clubhouse. "Who cares?"When reporters inquired about his cutter's lower velocity, Jansen harrumphed. Roberts was hurt by ongoing criticism of bullpen decisions and irritated by continuous queries about lineup building. Younger players, such as Cody Bellinger, Kiké Hernández, and Joc Pederson, were upset about losing at-bats in platoons. The unity of 2017 was gone.

The Dodgers did, however, return to the World Series, demonstrating how far Kershaw had fallen in the team's pitching hierarchy. To win the National League West, the Dodgers relied on Buehler in Game 163 against the Colorado Rockies. The Dodgers defeated Atlanta in the first round of the postseason, with Hyun-Jin Ryu starting Game 1. It took seven games to defeat Milwaukee and claim another National League pennant. The trophy came with an invitation to get throttled by the Boston Red Sox, who had 108 wins. "We did not expect to go to the World Series," Kershaw said. "I believe that was merely by default. "Nobody else was that good." The Red Sox annihilated him. Kershaw began Game 1 at Fenway Park on two days off after earning a save in Game 7 against Milwaukee. He gave up five runs over four innings. Kershaw pitched seven innings and allowed four runs in Game 5, which concluded the series. "Obviously, the Red Sox, I had nothing by the World Series," Kershaw said. "I was dead."

The defeat exposed all aspects of the organization to scrutiny. Roberts overheard Dodgers fans calling for his removal and read a scathing tweet from President Donald Trump criticizing his in-game strategy. The front staff failed to upgrade the bullpen at the trade deadline. The offense never materialized. There was little talk about whether Kershaw could win the big one. "This isn't a 'Kershaw in the playoffs' issue," one team official explained. "This is just a 'Kershaw in 2018' issue." The indictment has now stretched throughout the entire franchise: Why couldn't the Dodgers win the championship?

"It might not be a personal thing," Kershaw remarked after Game 5. "It might just be a 'play better' thing."

Kershaw eventually chose to opt out of his contract, but he never became eligible for free agency. He agreed to a three-year, $93 million agreement during the team's exclusive bargaining window following the World Series. The deal's brevity surprised many: Kershaw had been more vocal about the evil of tanking, which had carried the Cubs and Astros to the World Series while ruining many other organizations. He didn't like it when owners pretended to be poor. He still left money on the table, unwilling to test the market, wondering how his physique would deteriorate throughout a lengthier deal, and unsure how his spirit would falter if his talent weakened. "I think this year especially—maybe rightfully so—there's been a lot of people saying that I'm in decline or that I'm not going to be as good as I once was," Kershaw said after signing the contract. "I'm looking forward to proving a lot of people wrong with that."

Kershaw and Ellen had dinner with the McDaniels in Dallas on the night he signed the contract. McDaniel made four excursions to Highland Park that winter. McDaniel emphasized that Kershaw needs to be open to new ideas. Kershaw seems more willing to depart from his rigid approach to squats and running all the time. McDaniel focused on Kershaw's suppleness and flexibility, both of which were affected by back problems. McDaniel investigated Kershaw's ankle, hip, knee, and spine movement patterns. He studied golfers and tennis players, looking for any correlation that could help Kershaw improve his rotational force. McDaniel concentrated on Kershaw's core stability during his first trip to Texas. During the second journey, they strengthened the shoulder. On the third, they explored how to increase velocity. During the final visit, they analyzed how the elements merged together.

Kershaw appeared slimmer and more energized when he arrived at Camelback Ranch after his offseason. Team officials expressed cautious optimism. The emotion didn't stay long. Early in camp, his left shoulder ached. For the first time since 2010, the Dodgers needed someone other than Clayton Kershaw to start Opening Day. Roberts had signed a new deal during the offseason, but the team was entering a new chapter. Farhan Zaidi departed to lead the San Francisco Giants, but his impact on the team, such as signing Max Muncy, a lightly regarded first baseman who developed into an All-Star slugger, lasted. The atmosphere in the clubhouse seemed brighter. In the winter, the team eventually moved Yasiel Puig, whose behavior overshadowed his value at the gate. Yasmani Grandal left for free agency. When Kershaw made his debut in 2008, the organization re-acquired Russell Martin, the starting catcher. Martin tutored the future catcher, rookie Will Smith, during his final season in the majors. The clubhouse was full of native talent. That season, Bellinger hit 47 home runs while playing Gold Glove defense in center field, and he won the National League MVP. Buehler appeared to be an ace. There was additional talent on the way. Early in the season, Kershaw noticed that this bunch arrived at the ballpark sooner than any other club he had played for. "A lot of young guys," he answered, "who want lunch."

Andrew Friedman thought it was the best team he'd ever constructed. The Dodgers won 106 games, surpassing the previous record established in 2017. The lineup was dangerous, and the rotation was extensive. Buehler positioned himself as the confident tip of the spear. Ryu won the National League ERA title and was second in the Cy Young voting. Rich Hill had a 2.45 ERA. The abundance of skill decreased reliance on Kershaw—even if he still desired to bear the weight. The mounting burden of the postseason became clear to John Pratt, who spent hours in Kershaw's film room between starts. When the calendar switched to September, Pratt observed Kershaw's answers shortened and his patience lessened. On September 6, Kershaw appeared perplexed when Roberts pulled him after ninety-nine pitches midway through the fifth inning. "Why?" Kershaw inquired. In the dugout, he kicked a water cooler and yelled. He concluded the season with a 3.03 ERA, the tenth best among MLB starters but the worst since his rookie year. The offseason had not been a panacea. His fastball velocity has dropped from 90.9 mph in 2018 to 90.4 mph in 2019. And he still hung more sliders than he wanted.

However, while preparing the rotation for the first round against the 93-win Washington Nationals, the Dodgers made an unusual decision. Buehler won Game One. However, the team chose Kershaw for Game 2 over Ryu, who was the better pitcher in 2019. The argument indicated an organization torn between Kershaw's reality and his reputation. If the series went to a fifth game, Roberts stated before Game 1 that the Dodgers wanted Kershaw available to throw in relief.

The stage was set for calamity.

It should never have progressed that far.

On May 31, Washington was 19-31, 10 games back in the National League East, with a one-in-five chance of making the playoffs. The team won nine of its next eleven games, recovering from a nosedive to return to.500 by the end of June and punch a ticket to October with a 46-27 record in the second half—nearly matching the Dodgers' 46-24 pace. After defeating Milwaukee in the Wild Card game, Washington traveled to Los Angeles. The Nationals, a regular contender, papered over weaknesses with stars. Max Scherzer and Stephen Strasburg were among the top pitchers in baseball. Juan Soto had emerged as the game's best rookie hitter, a twenty-year-old with a remarkable eye and terrifying power. Anthony Rendon combined superb defense at third base with unexpected power. In a five-game series, the difference in depth between the two teams was only so significant. The stars would decide the series.

Buehler pitched six scoreless innings in the first game, but Strasburg out pitched Kershaw in the second. Kershaw gave up three runs in six innings, a great start but a disappointment. The hosts' talent did not wow the Nationals, nor did their strategies surprise them. "Our guys became too predictable in what we were calling," Honeycutt explained. A two-game split in Washington returned the series to Los Angeles for Game 5. The Nationals lined up Strasburg, who had built an impressive career despite never quite living up to the enormous hype that surrounded him after Washington drafted him first overall out of San Diego State in 2009. Strasburg never won a Cy Young Award and earned only three All-Star appearances. But he was outstanding in October. The match against Buehler was even. The Dodgers opened up a 3-0 lead with two home runs. Buehler kept the Nationals quiet until the sixth inning, when he allowed a run.

And that's when things turned weird.

As Buehler faced his first true test of the evening, Kershaw warmed up in the bullpen, hoping to repeat his relief performances from the previous three Octobers. The mere presence of Kershaw among the relievers was unusual. The Dodgers had, in Friedman's opinion, "the deepest bullpen we've had in terms of the number of options, the different looks." Instead of relying on that group, the team added Kershaw. Friedman later said that a starting pitcher "can be a really attractive bullpen option." Thus, the Dodgers ignored the foreshadowing. Kershaw had allowed a career-high twenty-eight home runs that season. In 2019, he had not thrown a fastball faster than 93 mph, which was his average in 2017. His first-inning ERA in 2019 was 5.79. Kershaw had a 5.24 ERA during six starts in August and September, allowing thirteen home runs. His left arm was killing him. "My shoulder hurt so bad," he said. When he lifted up to throw, it felt "like a knife." He didn't think he needed surgery, so he pitched through the pain. "I was like, 'I need to chill out,'" Kershaw explained. "But during the season, you can't chill out."

Rather than relaxing, Kershaw went on a rescue mission. Buehler had thrown 97 pitches, a total he had exceeded in less than half of his regular-season starts. Buehler, like Kershaw in previous postseasons, returned for the seventh inning, an ace asked to do just a little more. Buehler struck out one hitter and walked another before giving up the go-ahead run to left-handed outfielder Adam Eaton. Roberts rubbed Buehler's stomach and took the baseball. Kershaw loped in, head down, as "We Are Young" blared across Chavez Ravine. Unlike relievers who were asked to save him in previous years, Kershaw kept Buehler from suffering a tragedy. After Eaton failed to check his swing on a 0-2 slider, Kershaw pounded his glove and let out a shout.

"He emptied the tank against Eaton," Justin Turner remembered. "He experienced a massive adrenaline surge. The fans went crazy. He went crazy.

"And then…"

What happened next is still in contention.

Kershaw wrapped his left arm in a towel and moved to the end of the bench. The Nationals' two best hitters, Rendon and Soto, would bat in the eighth. The combination posed a logistical challenge for Roberts. Rendon batted from the right side, while Soto batted from the left. Behind Soto came two veteran right-handed hitters: Howie Kendrick and Ryan Zimmerman. Roberts had to select which of his relievers could handle the challenge. A couple of years ago, Roberts might have relied on Kenley Jansen for a two-inning save. However, Jansen's ERA has risen from 1.32 in 2017 to 3.71 in 2019, indicating a decline since the World Series. Adam Kolarek, a journeyman southpaw, may have been the best option for facing Soto. Soto was 0-for-3 against Kolarek during the series. "Kolarek is literally on the postseason roster to face Soto," Ross Stripling explained. But Roberts couldn't begin the inning with Kolarek facing a right-handed hitter like Rendon. Kenta Maeda, his greatest right-hander, had

CHAPTER 7
A HEAVY LOSS

*I*n the days following the World Series, Clayton Kershaw put on a brave face. The family gathered what they needed from their Studio City home and returned to Highland Park. He attempted to stay busy. He tried not to wallow. He attempted to overcome the most devastating professional failure of his life. None of this came easily.

"I saw how much that World Series, in particular, crushed him," Ellen told me. "It was so, so hard."

Kershaw did not always express his sadness. The youngsters cheered him up like nothing else could. But Ellen realized that when her husband became quiet, as if lost in meditation, he was attempting to digest what had happened, to figure out why he had fallen short yet again. "There's nobody who puts more pressure on himself than him," she told me. She was not the only one who noticed. Patrick Halpin described those months as "a very sensitive time at the Kershaws' house." His friends avoided talking about the Astros. "We didn't really want to talk about it," Halpin explained. "It was obvious that Clayton didn't want to talk about it."

The 2017 World Series might have been the joyful ending to Kershaw's postseason story. No one could witness Game 1 of that series, when Kershaw dominated Houston in the scorching heat, and call him a choker. The roller coaster of Game 5 tipped the scales against Kershaw. He had lost in a way that the public and he would never forget. He had become the uncommon baseball player for whom ESPN's First Take would dedicate a segment.

His friends and teammates complained about his bad luck, excessive consumption, and the failure of others around him. "If we had won pitched in both Games 3 and 4, and Roberts did not want him to face Soto. Julio Urías, a good lefty, was unavailable after throwing in Games 2-4.

So Roberts looked to the far end of the bench, where the best pitcher of his generation sat, his ailing arm covered in a towel. Kershaw was willing to continue pitching but did not expect to return for the eighth inning. He assumed his only assignment was Eaton. "Doc doesn't really say anything unless you're done," Kershaw explained. "He comes and tells you you're finished. So, if he doesn't say anything, keep going. So I just continued going." Roberts recalled the incident differently. "After he came back out, he goes, 'I want to get Rendon and Soto,'" Roberts recalled. Rick Honeycutt split the difference. "I remember [Kershaw] looking surprised when Doc said that he still had it," Honeycutt added. He gave a chuckle. "Looking back, you wish that wouldn't have happened."

So there was Kershaw, alone on the mound with a 3-1 lead, set up to fail. Rendon slouched in the batter's box, belying his brilliance. Many people in baseball believed Rendon didn't enjoy the sport. No one in baseball felt Rendon wasn't great at it. When Rendon enrolled at Rice University, the head coach asked his assistants, "Do you want to see Hank Aaron's wrists?"He held lightning in his hands.

Kershaw had planned to pitch with runners on base, so he continued pitching out of the stretch. Rendon missed a first-pitch curveball outside the zone. Will Smith asked for a slider. Kershaw extended his arms aloft. The pitch dropped below the strike zone. Rendon didn't care. He hit a home run beyond the left-field fence, reducing the advantage to one and leaving Kershaw shaking his head. "Rendon did a nice piece of hitting," Honeycutt said.

Kershaw circled the mound, and Rendon circled the bases. Soto walked up to the plate. Soto, who was only a few weeks away from turning twenty-one, was the youngest player on the field, but he could also have been the finest. That season, he became the first player since Frank Robinson to hit thirty home runs at the age of twenty. "Juan Soto just might be Ted Williams," the acclaimed baseball writer Jayson Stark remarked. Soto held a majestic posture at the plate, grinning and slithering around the box. He enjoyed nothing more than taking a close pitch, shuffling toward the pitcher, and retrieving his belongings. Soto reminded spectators that baseball is fundamentally about one man throwing a sphere and one man carrying a club.

There was no macho posturing vs. Kershaw. There was only one terrible pitch, a slider at Soto's belt, which Dodgers management later identified as arguably the worst Kershaw threw all season. Soto exploded the baseball. Kershaw crumpled on the mound. He removed his headgear. When he mustered the guts to turn around, the situation had already ended. The baseball landed almost a dozen rows deep in the right-center pavilion. 3-3.

All at once, the moment felt spectacular, incomprehensible, and completely predictable: it had happened again. Again. Again. How? What happens after 2013, 2014, 2016, 2017, and 2018? How could this have occurred again? When Kershaw accepted a new baseball from Smith, his shoulders crumpled, as if crushed by the weight of it all. Randy Wolf, a colleague from more than a decade ago, saw Kershaw as shattered. "I've just never seen that look on Clayton's face, when Soto hit that home run," Wolf remembers. "It was this look of disbelief, like, 'Are you kidding me?'" It was as if the strains and comments of previous postseasons had suddenly descended on him."

Kershaw would not pitch again in 2019. He looked like he never wanted to pitch again.

The TBS camera caught Kershaw alone in the dugout. The imagery expressed a deep melancholy. His forearms rest on his thighs. He looked at a floor covered in sunflower seeds and paper cups. Kershaw remained in that position for 75 minutes, which was enough time for the Dodgers to lose the game in ten innings. On occasion, he glanced up at the field. He would occasionally hold his head in his hands. He mostly looked down, overcome by the toxic combination of shame and disappointment. The camera followed him through the terrible end of another lost season, relaying his grief to friends, family, and former teammates.

If prior October collapses made it clear that fortune never smiled on Kershaw, this one was different. This one upset his teammates. "He went out there, did his job, and then had to go do more," Turner explained. "And it was all put on his back." That is what everyone is upset about. Because that contributed to the stigma of 'Oh, he's not performing in the postseason,' which is ridiculous. Stripling felt "heartbroken" for Kershaw. "You're kind of pissed at whoever made the decision to keep him out there, when we had what we had in the bullpen," Stripling remembers. Jansen was also worried. "I felt like it shouldn't be him," he explained. "If it should have happened, it should have happened to me." He continued, "I'm not blaming anyone. I adore the coaches. I adore Dave Roberts. I adore Andrew Friedman. But this should not be in Kersh's circumstance. That should be my situation." (Roberts said he did not regret sending Kershaw back out. "No," he said. "Because we talked about it. He was on board.")

The Dodgers threw their arms around their fallen ace in the clubhouse following the game. Will Smith expressed how much he admired Kershaw. Rich Hill burst into tears as he discussed Kershaw. Honeycutt, who would retire a week later, informed Kershaw that he cherished him. The words couldn't heal the wound. Kershaw made no excuses as he stood in front of reporters. He'd tried. He'd failed. He'd experienced this ache before. But he wasn't sure it had ever hurt so much. "Everything people say is true right now, about the postseason," Kershaw told the crowd. "I get that. There's nothing I can do about it right now. It is an awful feeling. When Daniel Hudson, a Dodger in 2018 and a happy National in 2019, saw Kershaw's interview, he said, "It was frickin' heartbreaking, to be honest with you." Matt Adams, a former Cardinal who spent 2019 with Washington, felt similar pity. "As any human being would with a good heart, you don't like to see the same stuff happening to the same guy, especially one of the best pitchers in history," Adams told me. (Not all Nationals felt sympathy; "There is no crying in baseball," Scherzer informed me.)

A. J. Ellis texted his support for Kershaw while watching from his home outside of Wisconsin. The game made him enraged, and that feeling never went away. "I'm still very angry about that," Ellis said. Ellis was more concerned with his friend's recovery than with tactical judgments.

CHAPTER 8
REINVENTION

Clayton Kershaw's phone was full of messages, which lifted his spirits just slightly as he mourned another lost season. A text message arrived from Paul Goldschmidt, the perennial All-Star first baseman. Goldschmidt, like Daniel Hudson, was moved by Kershaw's postgame comments. Goldschmidt believed he knew some of Kershaw's responsibilities. He lived beneath his own. "You feel that weight of the disappointment of not performing for your team, for your organization, for fans, for everything, and it weighs on you," Goldschmidt told me. "But sometimes how you handle failure speaks almost more about you than how you handle success." Goldschmidt chose to tell Kershaw "how much respect I had for him."

The baseball community treated Kershaw better than the media and the general public. (In a column following Game 5, I chastised the Dodgers for being "hopelessly wedded to the mythology of Clayton Kershaw.") Kershaw's teammates hailed him for pitching through pain. "He was playing through real injuries, hip, labrum, all kinds of stuff," J. says. P. Howell recalls. "I don't know what the specifics were regarding the injuries, but it wasn't a minor, three-day incident. It felt like, 'Hey, you should take six months off.'" They pondered why Max Scherzer and Justin Verlander, Kershaw's only true peers, avoided such scrutiny. "Those guys haven't had very much success in the postseason, either, and no one says anything about them," Justin Turner told me. "No one says anything about them. Like, hello?"

Kershaw often thought of Theodore Roosevelt's monologue about "The Man in the Arena." The first section of the speech—"It is not the critic who counts..."—was typically used by cantankerous athletes tired of the prying eyes of the press. But Kershaw was more concerned with the following statement, in which Roosevelt lauded the guy "whose face is marred by dust and sweat and blood; who strives valiantly; who errs, who comes short again and again," and who "if he fails, at least fails while daring greatly." That was Kershaw. He could handle the criticism if he could remain in the arena. "People come up to me and they make excuses," Kershaw said. "They say things like, 'Well, you shouldn't have pitched,' 'You shouldn't have come out of the bullpen,' and 'It wasn't right what they did. That would never happen anymore." All of this may be true. However, at the time, I was throwing and we lost. I failed. It hurt. It didn't feel great. It still does not feel well. But at the end of the day, I have no regrets about what occurred."

He continued, "Could Donnie have utilized me differently? Could Doc have utilized me differently? Or whatever it might be. They may have been able to defend me. But what player is going to get up here and say, 'Ah, I wish they protected me more'? That is the softest thing you could possibly say. "So you wear it."

A few days after Game 5, Brandon McDaniel paid Kershaw a visit in Los Angeles. "What should I do?" Kershaw asked McDaniel. Kershaw would turn thirty-two in April; he was no longer spray or indestructible, but he was far from old. Both men believed Kershaw could regain his fastball velocity and slider depth. "The frustration was, 'I know there's more in the tank, and I need to unlock it,'" remembers McDaniel.

Perhaps, McDaniel offered, an outside voice could help. He cited a pitching lab in Seattle's outskirts that did groundbreaking work. Kershaw had previously declined invitations. He was resistant to change, a stickler for history who believed a pitcher's record was more important than his spin rate. He was more concerned with throwing strikes and keeping runners in place than with motion-capture sensors and high-resolution cameras. But one slogan from the film adaptation of Moneyball stuck with him: "Adapt or die. When you're desperate for answers—or you just want to be back to what you were—you'll do a lot of stuff," Kershaw recalled. He advised McDaniel to schedule an appointment that would have seemed absurd only a few years ago.

Clayton Kershaw wanted to visit Driveline.

In the summer of 2012, when Kershaw was dealing with the hip injury that lost him the Cy Young Award, a twenty-nine-year-old college dropout named Kyle Boddy took a bus to Seattle to meet with Tampa Bay Rays management. For several years, Boddy had attempted to spark a revolution in the shadows of an industrial park near Sea-Tac Airport. According to The MVP Machine authors Ben Lindbergh and Travis Sawchik, Boddy believed that "baseball's entire minor-league and player-development structure needed to be rethought and rebuilt from scratch." He believed that by harnessing data, he could improve a pitcher's fastball and change the shape of his breaking ball. A Rays executive was fascinated by some of the concepts on Boddy's blog, Driveline Mechanics, and asked him to the team's hotel suite following a game versus the Mariners.

Boddy met Andrew Friedman, the future Dodgers manager. Boddy believed he might get a job. Friedman encouraged him to continue with the revolution. Boddy had a better chance of influencing baseball as an outsider. Lindbergh and Sawchik's book described how important he became. The game evolved in the 2010s as participants tapped into the knowledge of inquiring outsiders like Boddy—whose work experience includes Olive Garden waitress and PokerStars customer-service rep—rather than chaw-chewing, sun-poisoned locals. Boddy encouraged players to strengthen their arms by using weighted balls. He used high-speed cameras to study deliveries, collected biomechanical data, and proposed minor changes that resulted in huge improvements. "When you go watch the video, you can see the hair on your finger," pitcher Dan Straily told the New York Times in 2017. The detailed conversations were the point: Driveline attracted pitchers who wanted the microscopic edges that made the difference between millions and minor leagues.

Boddy butted into the industry, challenging its shibboleths. He kept around because his methods produced results. "You get some of these guys who were undrafted or late-round picks who are like test-tube babies—all of a sudden, they go into the pitching lab and they come out like Frankenstein, throwing like 100 mph," former Texas Rangers general manager Jon Daniels explained. As pitchers flocked to Driveline, the gospel spread. Boddy described his views in the book Hacking the Kinetic Chain. He preached to nonbelievers of all ages. When Bobby was speaking at Vanderbilt in 2015, a scrawny junior interrupted him. "I've read half of your book," Walker Buehler said, "and there's no fucking way anyone could do this." Boddy and Buehler discussed ideas for an hour. (To explain vertical rise, the mystery of the fastball that doesn't seem to descend, Boddy referenced Kershaw.) Buehler was further converted that summer, after the Dodgers took him in the first round, while recovering from Tommy John surgery. The Dodgers tasked Dr. James Buffi, who has a PhD in biomechanics and a Driveline internship, with developing Buehler's strength program. Buehler came from his talk with Buffi with more muscle and a regimen that contradicted Kershaw's.

"Walker's taught me a lot, honestly," Kershaw said. "Only about life. There are various approaches to doing tasks. The way he works and the way I work could not be more different." When Buehler first entered the rotation in 2018, the contrast perplexed Kershaw. "He works for, like, ten minutes a day," Kershaw explained. "He's a powerful person who lifts a lot of weight. incredibly quick-twitch, incredibly thin. Moves extremely rapidly. I'm this huge, old, chubby person who walks slowly and is in there forever." Over time, Kershaw realized that he should emulate Buehler rather than the other way around.

The Dodgers gave their athletes options for adaptation. The front office upgraded its facilities with cutting-edge Rapsodo and

Edgertronic cameras to analyze pitchers. They purchased Blast Motion sensors to measure swings. The Dodgers even erected a three-dimensional virtual reality lab inside their stadium. And they excelled at spotting failing players, pairing them with iconoclastic outsiders like Boddy, and reaping the rewards.

Kershaw was hearing a chorus of Driveline acolytes. For a while, he dismissed the unconventional methods and zealotry. "Earlier in my career, there's no way in hell I would have gone up there to do that," he told me. Then his friend Chris Young paid a visit to the facility following 2017. While playing catch with Kershaw that winter, Young responded to his friend's inquiries about the process. Brandon McCarthy went on a similar trek that offseason. Alex Wood recommended young Driveline employee Rob Hill. Kershaw pocketed the insight. "As you get hurt, you get more of an open mind," Kershaw said. "Or when your velocity starts to drop. When things aren't going well, you open up more."

His peers complimented the weighted-ball program and discussed fastball "vert" and shoulder-hip separation. Sometimes the language sounded strange. "He wants answers, and he does not want the long-winded version of that," McDaniel said. It was difficult for Kershaw to discuss his delivery. "Clayton never liked talking mechanics," Rick Honeycutt said. "He didn't want to hear me say mechanics.'" He liked the feel of the words above. "If I'm missing, I aim down," he once informed his colleague Stephen Fife. "If I'm missing right, I aim left." Kershaw threw each fastball as hard as he could. "I've got to be on top of the baseball, and you've got to be able to rip it down," he told me. He employed the simplest clues. "He always told me," Tony Watson remembered, "'The only thing I think about on my slider is down.'"

His adherence to the five-day cycle enabled this simplicity. "I've never played with any pitcher who executed the way he executed," Wood told me afterwards. Kershaw's regimen improved his delivery.

Mike Bolsinger, the pitcher for McKinney North High who knocked Highland Park out of the playoffs in 2006, went on to play in the majors for two seasons in Los Angeles. Bolsinger examined Kershaw's bullpens. At the end of the practice, Bolsinger noted the mound was immaculate. Kershaw's right foot constantly landed in the same location after each toss. "And then I'd see a rookie throwing and making a mess on the mound," Bolsinger recounted. Years later, Dodgers relief pitcher Caleb Ferguson discovered the same thing. "His repetition with everything that he does is so perfect," Ferguson recalled.

However, the five-day cycle has led Kershaw to disaster in 2019. His velocity had not been regenerated. His final two sliders of the season had hit the seats. "He got to a point where clearly something was not clicking," Mark Prior said. "So he needed to shock the system." Prior was a member of the evolving cast that will welcome Kershaw in 2020. Rich Hill and Hyun-Jin Ryu left for free agency. John Pratt departed the video room for the scouting department. Prior, a 2000s sensation whose career was derailed by injury, succeeded Honeycutt as pitching coach. Prior combined hard-earned experience with technical expertise. "We're not afraid to outsource things," Prior said. "If the message can be impactful coming from a different voice, so be it."

Before flying to Seattle, Kershaw texted A. J. Ellis. The journey surprised Ellis. Traveling to Driveline, Ellis said, illustrated how far Kershaw had fallen—and how much he had risen.

"That," Ellis told me, "was a massive moment of vulnerability for him—and openness."

Kershaw and McDaniel arrived in the industrial area near Sea-Tac eight days after Soto's home run hit the Dodger Stadium pavilion. The Driveline building was deserted except for a quartet of employees. The gang had been scrambling to prepare. Rob Hill was twenty-four years old and had recently finished his NAIA playing career. Now he was attempting to prolong the career of a first-ballot Hall of Famer. "It was one of those sorts of things that you can really only, like, dream about," Hill told me afterwards.

Kershaw felt closer to a fugue state. His body and spirits were in disarray. That winter, his shoulder would require a painkiller injection. Hill disrobed as he fitted motion-capture devices to his body. A staff member inquired about what music might motivate him. Kershaw sounded fatigued as he stood in his underwear, a little more than a week after his catastrophic defeat. "They were saying, 'Let's go! Let's throw your hardest!Kershaw recalled. "I said, 'You know what, guys? Whatever. I don't need it all." Kershaw reared back and fired as the cameras snapped and the computers recorded his information. He could barely reach 84 mph. "It was just painful to try to throw that hard," he explained.

Hill said the assessment sounded like gobbledygook. "The biggest pieces that came up were some of the stuff with his separation," Hill told me. "For example, the time when his upper and lower bodies began to create distance and torque. And those two, combined with their timing around foot plants, such as when the foot comes down. It also had an effect on where the arm was. He had become a little more open with his torso over the years. And then the arm went in some different areas." In layman's terms, once Kershaw damaged his back, his delivery shifted in ways that most people missed. "As you get older, you don't move as well," Prior explained. "You don't move as well as you did when you were 25. So, can you get them back into the roles, in a new way, so they can do what they used to?"While Kershaw consistently landed in the same location with each toss, the procedure to get there was incorrect. "The chain itself was firing in the right order," Hill recalled. "But the pieces weren't in the right place at the right times."

The analysis allowed Kershaw to rectify these flaws. The Driveline crew also convinced him of the benefits of weighted balls, which could strengthen his arm and help him regain velocity. At McDaniel's request, Kershaw added arm-care activities to his five-day schedule. Previously, he focused on preparation. Now he is focused on recovery. Kershaw knew his velocity would never be in the mid-90s again. He could live at 91-92 mph as long as the heater did not resemble the slider. His visit to the industrial park in Sea-Tac, the epicenter of a movement he had before regarded as frivolous, proved significant. He did not change his method or abandon the five-day cycle. But he did implement several tips into his regimen. The contrast would be startling. "Going up to Driveline lengthened his dominance," John Pratt said. "It led to this renaissance in the latter part of his career."

CHAPTER 9
AGAINST ALL ODDS

*T*he Las Colinas Resort bills itself as "The Essence of Texas Escapism." In October 2020, Clayton Kershaw and the rest of the Dodgers arrived at the facility, located in the center of the Dallas-Fort Worth metroplex, with their bags packed for a 26-day stay. The resort served as Major League Baseball's equivalent to the NBA's Covid-mandated bubble. All players, coaches, staff, and family members were provided rooms. If the squad kept winning, it wouldn't have to travel. The journey to the World Series passed via Texas.

For the Kershaws, the site was fortunate. The Melsons left supplies for the youngsters at the valet stand. The procedures prevented anyone inside the bubble from communicating with the outside world. However, the proximity to Highland Park allowed friends and family to attend postseason games, which were open to the public at a reduced capacity after being closed during the regular season. Leslie Melson may not have been able to watch the team otherwise. As October approached, Ellen said, the mother who had treated Kershaw as her fifth child was "in her weakest state. We basically had to carry her in," Jim Melson said. She was determined to see the Dodgers compete for a title. "This, truly, was as much her dream as it was Clayton's, for him to win a World Series," Ellen told me.

After settling into the bubble, the Dodgers swept the San Diego Padres in the first round of games at Globe Life Field. Kershaw pitched six innings of three-run ball in Game 2. Cody Bellinger climbed the center-field wall and stole a home run off Padres standout Fernando Tatis Jr. The final game was a 12-3 Dodgers victory, earning the team four extra days off before the next round.

On October 10, two days before the series start, Kershaw was throwing a bullpen session when a muscle in his lumbar region "kind of, like, gave out," he said. He stopped tossing as discomfort spread throughout his body. The diagnosis was less severe than prior injuries. Kershaw was suffering from back spasms that may be treated with a few weeks of rest. He did not have that much spare time. The team scratched him for Game 2. Kershaw listened as the medical professionals discussed alternatives. His best hope was a sequence of three injections in a row: Marcaine, cortisone, and Toradol, which would numb the area, battle inflammation, and relieve pain. "I'd never gone to those lengths before," he explained. "And I hope I don't have to again."

The staff delivered the trio of doses to see how they affected Kershaw's system. He played catch and threw a bullpen. "It was like, all right, it's okay," Kershaw recounted. The Dodgers lined him up for Game 4. By then, the Braves' fearsome lineup had propelled the team to a 2-1 series lead. If Kershaw could pitch like himself and avoid the demons that had tormented him so frequently in October, the series would be tied. On game day, Kershaw was given the three-shot cocktail again. This time, the mixture knocked him over. "When you have all that stuff, like, you just feel like a wet noodle out there, with no control of your body," Kershaw told me. His velocity dropped. He couldn't complete his slider. Everything felt weird. "You know that object at a car sale that's blowing in the breeze?"Kershaw recalled. That's kind of what I felt like."

Kershaw's shoulder-length hair fluttered as the wind blew through Globe Life Field's open top. Dirt swirled around, stinging the athletes. The setting seems spooky. For Kershaw, the location represented a familiar terror. Through five innings, his only blemish was a missed slider that Braves designated hitter Marcell Ozuna crushed for a solo home run. Everything collapsed in the sixth inning, when the score was deadlocked at one. Kershaw faced the top of Atlanta's lineup for the third time. Ronald Acuña Jr.'s infield hit sent Kershaw flying. Freddie Freeman, first baseman, doubled home Acuña on an inside fastball. Kershaw now bore full responsibility for the loss. With Ozuna up, Roberts remained with his injured ace. When Kershaw threw a full-count curveball, Ozuna hit an RBI double. Kershaw seems more resigned than shocked. For years, he had played the postseason patsy, the gunman who was outgunned in the end. He watched from the bench as the game went apart, resulting in a 10-2 loss.

After the game, Kershaw took his meds over Zoom. The session lacked the anguish of Game 5 against Washington. There was little to say; it looked that this man's lot in life was to go through these trials. Kershaw collapsed into his chair. He brushed his fingers through his hair. He gazed at the microphone. He appeared dejected. He trimmed his responses.

"With Ozuna there," Jorge Castillo of the Los Angeles Times remarked, "what were you trying to do with that pitch, on that double?"

"Get him out," Kershaw instructed.

He picked at the sleeve of his Dodgers hoodie. He didn't mention the injections, his lack of control over his body, or the weight on his shoulders following the October catastrophe. He boiled his evening down to its essence: he had tried again. Once again, he failed. His squad was one defeat away from being eliminated. Kershaw rode the bus back to the Las Colinas bubble. He was not scheduled to pitch again versus Atlanta.

He thought he could only pray for his colleagues to come through.

Then another thought occurred to him.

Rather than absorb the bitterness alone, Kershaw reached for his phone. He ignored his self-consciousness about leadership and sent a message to his teammates via their GroupMe thread. He reminded the players how talented they were. He encouraged them to remember that the series was not over. "Yeah," he said, "it's probably a little cheesy, sappy." But something about the note sparked the conversation. Messages came in throughout the night, from Turner, Bellinger and Hernandez, Joc Pederson, and Brusdar Graterol. Joe Kelly, a former Cardinal currently relieving for the Dodgers, assigned his son, Knox, to film an iPhone commercial about wanting to see fireworks the next night. Even Seager, a player so reclusive that Dodgers management used to lecture him on the need of supporting his teammates, got involved. "We just rallied around it, to come ready to play," Seager said.

For much of his career, when Kershaw stumbled in October, the rest of the Dodgers did as well. The offense batted.211 against St. Louis in 2013. A year later, when Matt Adams took Kershaw deep, the lineup did not respond. Daniel Murphy stole third base in 2015, and the defense fell asleep. The entire team fell against the 2016 Cubs before Kershaw did. Kenley Jansen blew Game 2 of the 2017 World Series, and the Astros crushed Yu Darvish in Games 3 and 7. In 2018, virtually no one turned up. The Dodgers should never have played an elimination game against the Nationals in 2019. Ellen wanted to howl when she read tales that solely blamed her husband. But she realized it was pointless and ineffective to assign blame for the losses. Kershaw had earned the burden. He had to carry it.

Those Dodgers teams lacked a key ingredient. None of them hired Mookie Betts. Betts saved the season in Game 5, a day after Kershaw's disappointing performance. The Dodgers were already down two runs in the third inning, with two runners on base. Dansby Swanson, the Braves shortstop, hit a line drive into right field. Betts caught the ball on his shoe-tops. In the process, Ozuna failed to correctly tag up at third base, resulting in a momentum-swinging double play, one of several gaffes made by Atlanta on the verge of the pennant. Two innings later, Will Smith hit the go-ahead home run against a Braves reliever named, uncannily, Will Smith. The Dodgers won 7-3, forcing Game 6, in which Buehler defeated Atlanta 3-1. On the penultimate night of the seven-day street brawl, Turner ended a Braves rally by diving to tag Swanson and whirling to complete a double play at third base. Bellinger hit the go-ahead homer in the seventh. Bellinger injured his shoulder after crossing the plate by leaping to bump forearms with Kiké Hernández. The Dodgers, who advanced to the World Series with a 4-3 win, could only injure themselves.

The Dodgers have assigned Clayton Kershaw Game 1 of the Fall Classic for the third time in four years. His opponent lacked the destructive force and name recognition of the 2017 Astros and 2018 Red Sox. In relative anonymity, the Tampa Bay Rays played modernist baseball, where form follows function. Only one of their position players, veteran outfielder Kevin Kiermaier, made an eight-figure wage. Only one of their regular batteries, first baseman Yandy Díaz, hit above .300. No Ray had pitched a complete game since 2016. Tampa Bay condensed baseball to its essence: how to score runs, how to stop runs, and the mathematical clockwork that underpins it. They positioned their defenders expertly. They layered their lineups expertly. They used their pitchers efficiently. The Rays played baseball like the Dodgers, which made sense considering Andrew Friedman's influence on both teams. The difference was that Friedman's new team paid for superstars like Kershaw and Betts. The Dodgers didn't need much else to win Game 1 8-3. Kershaw pitched six innings of one-run ball after loosening up his back. Betts sparked a rally with a walk and a stolen base in one inning before launching a home run in the next.

A large number of Kershaw's friends and family joined the thousands of fans inside Globe Life Field. Major League Baseball capped attendance at 11,500, leaving roughly three-quarters of the venue empty. Despite its small size, the gathering provided a welcome relief from the artificial hum of summer. Jim and Leslie Melson donned masks and went into the crowd. Ellen was unable to leave the family section, but she could still wave to her parents. "And that was as close as we got to them for that month we were in the bubble," she talked about. She maintained in touch with her husband's pals via a private text chain; every year in October, the group switched to a separate conversation where Ellen replaced Clayton. The majority of the Mean Street Posse still lived in Texas. They marveled at the coincidence of the postseason's venue. "It was the only way we could have seen him, being there at that time," Josh Meredith said.

When Kershaw went to the mound in Game 5, Ellen discovered the gang seven tickets above the first base line: Meredith, Ben Kardell, Patrick Halpin, Robert Shannon, Carter English, and the Dickenson twins were all nervous that night. They usually did whenever Kershaw pitched. Over the years, they had gone great distances to keep an eye on him. They had only experienced sadness during the postseason. And the 2020 World Series was headed that way, deadlocked at two games each. The Dodgers lost Game 4 in painful fashion, with the bullpen failing in three consecutive innings. In the ninth inning, with the Rays at first and second, Kenley Jansen allowed a single to journeyman outfielder Brett Phillips. One run was scored when center fielder Chris Taylor mishandled the ball. Randy Arozarena, a rookie star, took off from first base and ignored a stop sign at third. He would have been out had Will Smith not dropped the baseball and Jansen failed to back up the play. Arozarena dove home, pounding the plate with his palm. In the dugout, Roberts shouted, spit, and almost threw his cap. "It was like that imperfect storm," he explained afterwards. Roberts, ever the optimist, continued to look ahead. "Now it's a three-game series," he announced. "And we have Clayton going tomorrow."

Kershaw dressed unkempt to serve as a calming factor. His beard was mangy. Dirt soiled his cap, and sweat streaked the hair beneath it. The offense gave him a three-run lead in the second inning. Tampa Bay scored two runs in the third. An inning later, another unraveling appeared to be on the way. Kershaw walked speedy outfielder Manuel Margot. Margot advanced to second on the next pitch, beating out catcher Austin Barnes' throw. The ball bounced off Taylor's glove. Margot sneaked to third, 90 feet from tying the game with no outs.

At his core, Kershaw realized that not all outs were equal. He tailored his attack to meet the needs of his team. If the Dodgers needed a strikeout, a double play, or a speedy inning, he could do it without saying how. Brandon McCarthy and Zack Greinke used to call it "magic. I think natural run suppression is some sort of an innate gift, at some level," McCarthy told me later. Or, as Ross Stripling described it, "He just out-competes you, man." With Margot at third, the Dodgers' needs became evident. Kershaw couldn't let him score. He walked the next batter, outfielder Hunter Renfroe, before infielder Joey Wendle came to the plate. Kershaw trapped Wendle with an inside fastball for a single. Margot stayed put. Kershaw knocked out shortstop Willy Adames with a pitch. Margot began to feel antsy. With Kiermaier up, Dodgers first baseman Max Muncy observed Margot feinting toward home plate, as if attempting to time Kershaw's delivery.

As a left-handed pitcher, Kershaw turned his back on third base. He looked over his right shoulder to check on Margot, but then he raised his arms to the sky, sighed, and gathered himself before throwing. Muncy's duties included guarding Kershaw's blind side. Kiermaier fouled off the first pitch. Barnes returned the baseball. Kershaw caressed it in his hands and looked at Margot. When Kershaw raised his arms, Margot rushed off. He was attempting to steal home in the

World Series, a remarkable display of audacity. Muncy charged forward, pointing at the plate and yelling across the diamond. "Home! Home! Home!"A play like this did not come up frequently in preparation meetings. The players did not practice during the season. For a split second, when Margot sprinted to the plate and Kershaw detected the sneak attack, the Dodgers' fate was decided by a battle of moxie and innate instincts.

Greg Maddux liked Kershaw's attention to all aspects of the game, even as a rookie. Kershaw cared about more than simply pitching. He cared about winning baseball games. He cared about his at-bats. He was concerned about fielding his position. He was also concerned with keeping the running game under control. When Muncy pointed, Kershaw reacted with amazing control, sliding his left foot behind the mound to avoid a balk, which would have given Margot the run. "He's so aware of everything," Muncy explained. "He knew exactly what he was supposed to do." Kershaw, straddling the rubber, passed the ball home. Barnes stepped in to catch the baseball and tag Margot, who was inches away from tying the game. The umpire punched his fist. Kershaw pumped his own. In the dugout, he discovered his first baseman. "Hey," Kershaw said to Muncy, "nice job."

Kershaw did not allow another batter to reach base throughout his 4-2 triumph. He had more issues corralling Cali and Charley as they swarmed all over him while he was doing his postgame Zoom. "You guys are maniacs," he continued. He smiled. He made five starts in the longest and oddest postseason of his career, posting a 2.93 ERA. The Dodgers won four of these games. And now he was just one triumph away from salvation.

Matt Gangl walked across the loading dock outside Globe Life Field on October 27, opened the door to a production van, and sat in his chair in front of a wall of monitors. Gangl, the lead director of Fox's MLB coverage, had occupied that seat sixteen times in the previous twenty-two days, while remaining in quarantine. When he checked into his Dallas hotel four weeks ago, he asked for a room with a microwave and a refrigerator. He survived on supplies from a neighboring Whole Foods Market and catered lunches at the game. "It was a little surreal, when you're doing the same thing, every day, driving the same path," he told me.

His preparation for that day was slightly different. Gangl and his crew brainstormed options for covering a Dodgers victory celebration during Game 6. The franchise hadn't won the World Series since 1988. Fox trusted Gangl to nail the moment. He devised nearly two dozen methods to isolate specific cameras. He assigned a camera to Dave Roberts in the dugout. He focused a camera on Magic Johnson, the most well-known member of the Guggenheim group, in the stands. And he sent a camera to follow the player who had become a symbol of this team's excruciating pursuit of a championship.

"One of the key ones," Gangl said, laughing, "was going to be having something on Mr. Kershaw."

Kershaw was not scheduled to start either Game 6 or 7, so he offered to pitch from the bullpen. The night before Game 6, he told Ellen, "If they need me, I'll be there." She spent the whole evening wondering if her husband would appear relieved. Sitting along the first base line behind the Dodgers' dugout, she alternated between the action on the field and the relievers roaming about the bullpen. Higher up in the stands, Kershaw's friends experienced "an incredible amount of stress," Halpin said. He continued, "There was also a sense of 'How is this going to fall apart again?'"

Game six was a minor-key classic. Arozarena blasted a single homer in the first inning. In the second inning, Roberts turned to his bullpen. He pressed button after button, relying on unheralded relievers like Dylan Floro, converted starters like Alex Wood, and despised veterans like Pedro Báez. Blake Snell, the Rays starter, was pitching the game of his life. Through five innings, he has struck out nine and allowed only one hit. Snell, a twenty-seven-year-old lefty, epitomized the new pitching era, from which Kershaw drew inspiration. Snell earned the 2018 American League Cy Young Award despite failing to complete the eighth inning all season. He was great at missing bats and not finishing games. His performance dropped when he faced hitters for the third time. Prior to Game 6, he had never made it past the sixth inning in sixteen appearances in 2020. Barnes doubled up the middle on Snell's seventy-third pitch, with one out in the sixth inning. Kevin Cash, the Rays manager, did not hesitate. He eliminated Snell from the game.

The decision became a flashpoint in the long-running argument over baseball's shifting landscape, prompting roundtable discussions and lectures from Bob Costas about the game's disappearing heartbeat. The Rays made decisions based on analytical horsepower. Cash believed, based on mountains of statistics, that one of his relievers would do better against the following batter than Snell. He believed he was making the correct decision. He believed it months later, even though he was still torn over the issue. Finally, it may not have mattered which pitcher Cash chose to face the next batter. The next batter was Mookie Betts.

Betts didn't waste time. He hit a double off reliever Nick Anderson. Barnes scored after Anderson threw a wild pitch. When Seager grounded out, Betts raced home for the winning run. Roberts asked Julio Urías, a 24-year-old lefty, to collect the final seven outs. Roberts maintained his calm as pandemonium reigned in the dugout. Before the top of the eighth inning, an MLB official approached

Justin Turner, who had tested positive for Covid. Turner dashed inside a room behind the dugout while his teammates speculated about his disappearance. Betts finished his outstanding first season as a Dodger by hitting a home run in the bottom of the eighth. Kershaw paced through the bullpen. For once, he had little cause for concern. Urías sped through the ninth. The final pitch of the 2020 season was a 97-mph fastball that hit the inner half of the plate for a called third strike. Urías reared back and yelled. Barnes grabbed the baseball, threw his glove and mask, and sparked a mosh pit. The players jumped over the dugout railing, ran in from the outfield, and barreled out of the bullpen. For a few seconds, while the photos were flashed around the country, one man was absent.

Ross Stripling was no longer with the Dodgers. That July, the team traded him to Toronto. As he watched at his in-laws' Houston home, he posed the question that had been on many people's minds.

Logan White found the 2020 postseason bittersweet. The resentment originated from the Dodgers' early-round elimination of San Diego, which employed White as an executive. The pleasure arose as Kershaw checked off the final box on his Hall of Fame resume. "It was off the charts awesome," White remembered. (White was not the only former Dodgers official to shed tears; Ned Colletti, commentating for the team's television network, did as well.) It was easy for White to become emotional when discussing Kershaw, reminiscing about catching that preseason scrimmage with his old teammate Calvin Jones, or reflecting on his failure to sign Luke Hochevar the year before the 2006 draft. He saw himself as a mere instrument in a divine sequence. "I'm not sure I did much, if you really want to know the truth," he told me afterwards. "It was all destined. "Everything was planned out."

Over the years, Mark Lummus, the Mariners scout who initially noticed Jones' work with Kershaw, ran into White at games. The patriotic Texan was filled with envy. "I just had to look at him like,

'Goddamn. "You signed the greatest pitcher to ever come out of my state," Lummus said.

When Lummus taught inexperienced scouts, he cited Kershaw as an example: "He's in the textbooks: 'This is what we're trying to find, boys.'" The scouts needed to learn as much as they could about what inspired these players. Did they aspire to greatness? Did they realize what greatness entailed? It was less about the delivery, spin rate, and body type. It was about the brain, spine, and heart. Was the heart beating for this?

"He exhibited those characteristics back then," Lummus said. Logan White saw them. And the rest of us probably didn't view them in the same way Logan did.

The players passed around the trophy, which had not belonged to the Dodgers since 1988. When Kershaw held the trophy, he smiled "like he's holding his firstborn," according to Rick Honeycutt. Honeycutt was standing in a suite next to Tommy Lasorda. Honeycutt retired and worked as a consultant with the Dodgers, but he was unable to break through the bubble. He screamed and whistled at his old students. He witnessed pleasure on the faces of Kenley Jansen, Alex Wood, and, of course, Kershaw.

Kershaw felt "like a son to me," Honeycutt said. He had mentored Kershaw through his adolescent years, into popularity, and through heartbreak. "Getting someone at such a young age, you almost felt like he was part of you," Honeycutt told me. Kershaw had a similar affinity. He felt uneasy referring to anyone as a father figure. But he was thankful for Honeycutt. "He's a guy who is always in your corner," Kershaw explained. "I'm really thankful I got to have him."

"If I had a daughter, before he got married, I would have been pushing my daughter his way," Honeycutt told me afterwards. "Because he is the kind of person you can trust. "I just loved every

111

aspect of his being."

A few players stuck around for Zoom interviews. Betts, a two-time winner, spoke as if this were any other day at the office. "I was traded to help get us over the hump," he told me. "I used that as fuel," Kershaw said, looking ecstatic. "I've been saying 'World Series champs' over and over in my head, just to see if it will sink in," he told reporters. He brushed away a question about his postseason legacy, unable to express the relief he was still experiencing.

"Those are all bad questions, man—I don't care about any of that," Mr. Kershaw replied. "We've won the World Series." I do not care about legacy. I'm not concerned about what happened last year. I don't care what others think. I don't care, guy. We've won the World Series. The 2020 Dodgers won the World Series. Who cares about all the other stuff? To be a member of that team—all of the other stuff is worthless. It does not matter. "We won."

At his Wisconsin home, inside The House That Kershaw Built, A. J. Ellis watched a triumph bigger than the ones he had spent his whole summer reliving.

"I'll never forget just sitting on the couch, just smiling, watching him run in," Ellis told me afterwards. "Looking to the heavens. He smiled. As cliché as it may sound, you can see it all coming off his back as he raced. It was quite special for my pal."

The two men exchanged texts that night. A day later, Ellis called to tell his old partner how delighted and proud he was for Clayton and Ellen. "She's walked hand-in-hand with him throughout his entire career," Ellis said, "and through all of the traumatic October experiences." The championship did not belong solely to Kershaw. It belonged to his whole family.

In January, as the end approached, the Melsons crowded around Leslie. She reached for the hand of the youngster she had raised as if he were her own son. Clayton Kershaw had come to her door over twenty years ago as a pudgy youngster with the number 52 shaved into the side of his skull, an only child whose own house was frequently empty. Leslie had fed him, dressed him, and welcomed him on vacation, exposing his eyes and emotions to the love of a family. She had prepared him for his departure to Dodgertown and the world of professional baseball. She had seen him mature into a man, husband to her youngest daughter and father to her grandkids. She had watched him fail at his craft and then rise again year after year.

She had suffered alongside him. She wanted him to understand that.

"We did it," Leslie stated.

Kershaw was puzzled. Leslie held his hand and repeated herself.

"We did it," she yelled. "We won a World Series."

CHAPTER 10
LEGACY ON HIS TERMS

*K*ershaw had been planning his exit strategy since his first contract extension. In 2013, he turned down a fifteen-year, $300 million contract since the terms seemed limitless. After the Dodgers won the World Series in 2017, Kershaw hinted at a fitting sendoff. "If we win, I might retire," Kershaw explained. "I might just call it a career." Sandy Koufax retired at the age of thirty. Kershaw was 32 when the Dodgers won in 2020. He chose to promote his leaving method.

After the 2021 season, Kershaw will be a free agent. He informed Jorge Castillo of the Los Angeles Times that he expected to sign a one-year contract. He presented himself with an annual three-pronged crossroads: he could sign with the Dodgers, sign with his hometown Rangers, or retire. The candor was welcome, especially from Kershaw, who acted as if updates on his health required a security clearance. Kershaw sometimes regretted being so upfront about his ambitions. It gave people the right to ask him about retirement. And he had no intention of treating his appearance on the diamond as a gift.

"I feel like I might be guilty of this sometimes, talking pretty casually about retirement," Kershaw said to me at Camelback Ranch. "I feel like that disrespects those who work hard just to stay in the major leagues. I don't ever want to appear ungrateful. I continue to like playing baseball. And that is essentially why you are still here. I adore the game. It's a pleasant feeling to know that you have some influence over when you'll call it a career."

He had tried to keep control as he approached his mid-thirties. The nature of his quest shifted following the title. And so did his status in the Dodgers' hierarchy.

In the spring of 2021, I called Kershaw to ask him a specific question I'd been thinking about since he won the World Series. Some baseball fans discounted the importance of winning a title after only sixty games. "Somewhere deep down inside, I was a little bit happy" when Kershaw won, Madison Bumgarner said. "And was also happy that it came in 2020—so I can say, 'It might not count.'" For Kershaw, it did. Kershaw blasted Queen's "We Are the Champions" for weeks after winning the championship, loud enough that neighbors could hear it when they walked by, and frequently enough that his children became tired of the song.

The Dodgers never participated in the typical post-title ceremonies. The pandemic left the country paralyzed. There was no parade. When the players received their championship rings in April, a throng of 15,036, the maximum capacity for Dodger Stadium, congratulated them. It was up to each individual to contextualize their achievement. Not everyone was happy. Justin Turner felt scapegoated for taking team photos after testing positive. Kenley Jansen was upset because he had not been trusted to record the last outs. Walker Buehler couldn't wait to win again at a packed stadium and bask in the glory of victory.

So I was intrigued how Kershaw would react when I called.

"Are you feeling happier now?" I asked.

For a brief period of time, the air was silent.

"I don't think that's a fair question," the man replied.

He had a life outside of fastballs and sliders, the rigors of the first four days, and the strain of the fifth day. Later that year, at their Los Angeles home, Ellen threw Clayton a baseball. She had inked the number four between the seams. "And he was playing with it, as he normally is, when he glanced at it and said, 'What?'" Ellen recalls. Their fourth child, a boy called Chance James Kershaw, was born in December. Cali and Charley had started school, and Cooper needed to be monitored at home. Kershaw was no longer a carefree young guy whose only responsibilities were his wife and his trade. At times, baseball engulfed him. To the majority, it defined him. However, he could not describe his existence as just a pursuit for a title.

"If I said yes to that," Kershaw added, "that'd be like... losing in the playoffs is my only reason for living." And this is not true. I think my personal and family lives have been wonderful. I've had a great time with my kids and family, regardless of what happens in baseball."

He'd never pictured himself as Sisyphus. But it felt good to leave the boulder atop the hill. He was overwhelmed by the number of texts he received following the World Series. He never asked his teammates or friends to feel sorry for him. Only after he won did he realize they "really felt that pain I was going through," he explained. He had assumed that only Ellen shared the strain. The championship washed over him in waves. First there was relief. Then there was bliss. Then he realized how much his win meant to others. "Just to see how many people were happy for me, man, I was like, 'Man, that's awesome,'" Kershaw told ESPN. "I felt happy. So that was wonderful."

He was nearing the end of his professional journey. During the spring, Dave Roberts named Kershaw the team's Opening Day starter, an honor he had missed in 2019 and 2020 due to injury. Kershaw was not considered the Dodgers' number one pitcher. Walker Buehler was in front of him. The organization anticipated Julio Urías would replace him at the top of the rotation. There was also a new player on the club, one with a rich contract and a contentious reputation.

Trevor Bauer, a right-handed pitcher who grew up in a Los Angeles suburb, was one of baseball's most significant players in the first two decades of the 21st century. He became synonymous with Driveline, refining his weapons in the pitch-design laboratory and spreading the word to anyone who would listen. He also discovered a technique to convey other ideas to people who didn't always want to listen. He was a blossoming content developer who irritated people on social media. He engaged in a range of ill-advised online behaviors, including transphobic comedy, birtherism, and misrepresenting of indigenous people's opinions. The most distressing aspect was his harassment of people on social media, particularly women. He frequently responded to those allegations, which were documented in his own tweets, with fury that his character was being attacked.

Bauer's early career was fraught with errors. After the Arizona Diamondbacks traded him in 2012, less than two years after selecting him with the third choice in the draft, catcher Miguel Montero stated that Bauer "never wanted to listen" to instructions. His performance in the 2016 postseason with Cleveland was hampered by a drone accident that left him with an injured finger. After a rough performance in 2019, Bauer whirled around and threw the ball over the center-field fence as manager Terry Francona approached to pull him. Bauer's performance peaked in 2020, when he won the National League Cy Young Award with Cincinnati. His timing was perfect, since he entered free agency that winter. Andrew Friedman had been messaging members of his front staff, "Let's be pigs." He didn't want the team to rest on its laurels after winning one championship. So Friedman indulged in ugly gluttony. He authorized Bauer's signing to a three-year, $102 million contract in February 2021. At a press conference that month, Friedman defended the team's screening of Bauer. He emphasized that the new pitcher "is going to be a tremendous addition, not just on the field, but in the clubhouse, in the community."

Less than five months later, on June 29, a lady applied for a temporary domestic violence restraining order against Bauer in Los Angeles County Superior Court. The lady claimed Bauer strangled and punched her during sex without her consent. Bauer rejected the claim and eventually filed a defamation case against her. The woman's restraining order request was denied, and Los Angeles prosecutors decided not to seek charges against Bauer. However, after the Dodgers placed Bauer on administrative leave on July 2, during which he continued to be paid, other accusers came forward with similar allegations. Major League Baseball issued a two-year punishment, which was ultimately reduced by an arbitrator to 194 games. Bauer never pitched for the Dodgers again. Following Bauer's suspension, the Dodgers released him in the spring of 2023. Bauer spent his season pitching in Japan.

The Bauer case put a cloud over the Dodgers throughout the summer of 2021. Team officials avoided inquiries about him. The players were stumped on what to say. Kershaw maintained he didn't know Bauer very well. He praised Bauer's pitching knowledge. But their schedules didn't coincide, he explained. "He was fine inside the clubhouse," Kershaw recalled. "He was on his own a lot, did things at different times than everyone else, worked out at different times," Kershaw complained of Bauer's content-creation machinery. "He filmed stuff in the clubhouse, which I never really liked," Kershaw explained. "But, like, overall, I didn't have a bad experience with him." Even in the winter of 2023, as Bauer and the first accuser waged a yearlong flurry of claims and countercharges, Kershaw wasn't sure what to say about his former colleague.

"I always think it's a good idea to have the legal process [MLB's process] run its course before jumping to any conclusions about what you read about," Mr. Kershaw said. "At the same time, I can see how it was a major distraction for everyone. And Trevor's unabashed approach to the situation undoubtedly made things more difficult.

That was a little challenging. But we still coped with it.

A rainstorm halted Kershaw's appearance at Nationals Park on July 3, a day after the Dodgers paid a visit to President Joe Biden in the White House. Kershaw sat in the dugout, a towel over his left arm. He rubbed the sweat off his brow and tried to ignore the discomfort.

"That whole season, my elbow hurt," Kershaw recounted. "Probably starting in May. And then it eventually failed in July."

The Dodgers put him on the injured list four days later. The public diagnosis was forearm discomfort, but the injury was more severe. Kershaw had ripped a part of the flexor tendon that connects his arm and elbow. It wasn't his ulnar collateral ligament, which was repaired with Tommy John surgery. However, it was still his first severe elbow injury. The medical personnel believed he could avoid surgery if he rested. Kershaw missed July, August, and the first two weeks of September. To compensate for Kershaw's uncertainty and Bauer's absence, Friedman made a trade deadline splash, acquiring Washington Nationals ace Max Scherzer as well as former All-Star shortstop Trea Turner.

Kershaw pushed to return for the postseason. On September 13, he returned to pitch 89 mph fastballs in a victory over Arizona. "There's not a lot of better feelings in the world than getting to pitch here and getting a win," Kershaw informed the crowd. The feeling wouldn't stay long. On October 1, with only three games remaining in the regular season, he was attempting to finish the second inning against Milwaukee at Dodger Stadium when he felt another piece of his elbow fail. Roberts and a member of the training staff exited the dugout. After a brief talk, Roberts placed his hand on Kershaw's lower back and led him off the mound. The startled audience gave an ovation. Kershaw walked off the field with the baseball in his left hand, a symbol for anybody looking for one after hinting at retirement earlier in the season.

"Just an accident," Kershaw said. "I knew I didn't blow out."

But his season had ended. He watched from the dugout as the 106-win Dodgers won a thrilling National League Division Series over the 107-win San Francisco Giants, only to run out of gas against the 88-win Atlanta Braves in the following round. The Braves avenged last year's disaster by defeating the Dodgers on route to the World Series. The Dodgers had scheduled Scherzer to start Game 6 against Atlanta. After throwing four times in twelve days, including a bullpen appearance against San Francisco, Scherzer described his arm as "overcooked." The Dodgers scratched him. Buehler threw Game 6 in Scherzer's absence on short rest for the second time in two weeks and was hammered.

A month later, Scherzer agreed to a three-year, $130 million contract with the New York Mets. In 2022, Buehler had Tommy John surgery for the second time.

"I'll always respect Walker for pitching that game," Kershaw reflected. "We lost, he allowed a home run, whatever. "He took the ball."

That winter, Kershaw faced his first three-pronged decision: Dodgers, Rangers, or retirement. The Dodgers gave him room and declined to make a one-year, $18.4 million qualifying offer, which is often used as a precursor to free agency for most big-name players. That means the team would not receive draft-pick compensation if he signed elsewhere. However, the qualifying offer would have needed to be accepted or rejected within a two-week period, and Friedman did not want to rush Kershaw.

Kershaw needed the time. His elbow remained damaged. He disliked washing his hair or signing his name. By December, he was unable to secure a deal. Major League Baseball's thirty owners locked out the players on December 1 due to disagreements over a new collective bargaining agreement. The standoff lasted ninety-nine days, during which players and teams could not interact. Kershaw tested his arm in Highland Park High's indoor facilities. His elbow continued to hurt, but the discomfort soon subsided. "If I picked up a ball in January, [and] it was like, 'I need surgery,' and had to miss the next year, I don't know what that would have looked like," he told me.

At least one Ranger official spent the lockout concerned about Kershaw's health. The previous year, Texas hired Chris Young, a former All-Star pitcher and fellow Highland Park local, as general manager. Young wants the opportunity to sign his former offseason throwing partner. The Rangers underlined the seriousness of their rebuilding attempts by paying nearly $500 million for two infielders, Marcus Semien and Corey Seager, the 2020 World Series MVP, whom they enticed from Los Angeles with a ten-year, $325 million contract. If Kershaw requested a multiyear contract, the team was eager to provide him one. "There was a sense that it had a real possibility," said one source acquainted with the discussions.

Kershaw shattered the Rangers' hopes when the new CBA was ratified on March 10. "As soon as the lockout ended, I received a phone call that broke my heart," Young told me. "But I completely understand it." Kershaw agreed to a one-year, $17 million contract with Los Angeles in 2022. He announced the change on Instagram, writing, "We're back!"

The reason he returned became clear during his first game of 2022, against the Minnesota Twins on a 38-degree day at Target Field.

Kershaw dominated his inexperienced opponents. He struck out thirteen. He allowed no hits. He issued no walks. He didn't hit any batters. He kept the bases clean for seven flawless innings and eighty pitches, more than he had thrown in any of his previous appearances during the lockout-shortened spring training season. After the seventh inning, Roberts and pitching coach Mark Prior came in to relieve him. He left his attempt at the twenty-fifth perfect game in baseball history unfulfilled. "Blame it on the lockout," Kershaw stated that day. "Blame it on me not picking up a baseball until January."

He was more concerned with the Dodgers' long-term success than with his own personal successes. Some of his buddies disagreed with him. A. J. Ellis called to shout at him the following day. "We would have known the answer in fourteen pitches or less," Ellis informed Kershaw.

"I probably regret it now," Kershaw remarked. "I believe pitching a perfect game would have been fantastic." He continued, "Doc, he wanted to take me out. Mark wanted to take me out so badly. I could do what I always do: make things extremely difficult for them and stress them out. Or simply take it. So I just took this. Looking back, I regret it. "I should have tried."

He was moving into a nicer, gentler phase of his profession. There was a sense of relaxation that had been missing before the Dodgers won the championship. Prior to Kershaw's start in 2021, he crossed paths with Seager, who followed protocol and kept silent. Seager was taken aback when Kershaw looked at him and said, "Hey. Oh my God. What is happening?" Seager recalled. Kershaw relaxed in pre-start meetings. "You might still get a bit on the hand," Austin Barnes explained. "But that's okay." Through word and deed, he provided parenting advice to his younger teammates. One of Cody Bellinger's favorite memories from Los Angeles was witnessing Kershaw cradle Bellinger's daughter during a card game. "He makes everyone look bad—he's just Super Dad," Joc Pederson stated. In 2022, Kershaw became close to new teammate Tyler Anderson, whom Kershaw had criticized years before for delaying a game because Anderson finished his pre-start bullpen session late while pitching for the Colorado Rockies. "I would call him 'the Oracle' or 'the North Star,'" Anderson remembered. "Whatever he did, I would follow suit. He makes the correct decision every time."

Kershaw used a delicate but forceful touch to get the newest Dodger out of his depression in June. Freddie Freeman had made five All-Star teams and won the MVP award as the Braves' first baseman. After Atlanta won the World Series, Freeman planned to re-sign and end his career there. So he was surprised following the lockout when general manager Alex Anthopoulos, who had worked with Friedman in Los Angeles for two seasons, decided to trade for Matt Olson, a younger and less expensive substitute. Freeman signed a six-year, $162 million contract with the Dodgers, hardly a consolation prize. However, his disbelief took months to wear off. He remained apart from his new teammates. When he returned to Atlanta for the first time, he cried at a news conference and again during a standing ovation from Truist Park. His continuous waterworks were the subject of clubhouse discourse. In an article about the Dodgers-Braves rivalry published in the Atlanta Journal-Constitution, Kershaw mentioned Freeman's reception and subsequent emotion. "I hope we're not the second fiddle," Kershaw added. "We have a really good squad over here, too. I believe he will appreciate it once he feels at ease here." The statement went viral on social media. Freeman received the message. Following the series, he texted the Dodgers to express his gratitude for their patience. He began to open up to his teammates. His friendship with Kershaw has improved. Kershaw valued Freeman's dependability. "Just the fact that he goes and plays every single day, and doesn't want to come out, you can use that to the benefit of the team," Kershaw said in 2009. "That changed my opinion on him a little bit."

Also in June, the Dodgers eventually persuaded Sandy Koufax to allow the franchise to display a statue of him outside Dodger Stadium. He hadn't thrown a pitch since 1966, but his influence was still felt throughout the organization, thanks in part to the southpaw the Dodgers invited to speak at the ceremony. On his way to Joe Torre's charity event in 2010, Kershaw recalled how his friendship with Koufax began. He tried to express the significance of knowing that a man like Koufax cared about him. When famed announcer Vin Scully retired, Kershaw informed the audience that Koufax said, "The thing I appreciate most is he allows me to call him buddy." Kershaw stumbled through his next words: "That's the same for me. I'm grateful for that, Sandy, and I know you don't believe it, but no one deserves this distinction more than you."

A month later, Dodger Stadium hosted the All-Star Game for the first game since 1980. As part of the festivities, Kershaw was named the National League's starting pitcher for the first time. Before accepting the assignment, he considered the National League's greatest pitcher that season, Sandy Alcántara of the Miami Marlins, a lithe, six-foot-five right-hander. Like Kershaw in his teens, Alcántara believed in finishing games. Alcántara was one of the few pitchers still given that opportunity. He played six complete games in 2022, tying Kershaw's career high from the MVP season of 2014. Kershaw requested Alcántara's phone number from his former Marlins manager, Don Mattingly. When Kershaw called, he apologized. He told Alcántara that he was thinking about retiring and might never receive another chance to start the Midsummer Classic. Alcántara told Kershaw that he wouldn't protest. "He called me because he knew I deserved it," Alcántara explained. "I respect him a lot."

On the day of the game, Kershaw alternated between enjoyment and his customary pre-game ritual. When Pederson entered the training room, he was already seated at his Giants All-Star table. "What are you doing?"Kershaw said. Pederson left the room, laughing.

Kershaw noticed Giants traveling secretary Abe Silvestri, a former visiting clubhouse manager. "He gave me the sweatiest, nastiest hug," Silvestri remarked. Before his first pitch, Kershaw stepped off the field and gazed up at Elysian Park, which was surrounded by a sea of fans. Kershaw struck out Yankees star Aaron Judge and Angels sensation Shohei Ohtani in a scoreless inning. He also did something unusual on the baseball field: he had fun.

The dream did not last long. Sixteen days later, Kershaw's back seized. He was absent for about a month. He made only 22 starts in 2022. He hadn't made 30 starts since 2015. During those years, he only topped 175 innings. He pitched 1,503.1 innings in his first seven complete seasons, but only 970 in the following seven. The rigors of the cycle, combined with the violence of the fifth day, had reduced him to a highly competent part-timer. He could no longer perform the tasks he formerly did.

However, no one else could.

Kershaw, who was twenty-two years old at the time, was one of forty-five pitchers to surpass 200 innings, the current measure of a pitcher's longevity. In 2021, only four pitchers reached 200. The total rose to eight in 2022 before dropping to five in 2023. The expectations for pitchers had shifted. The industry had learnt the dangers of facing an opposing lineup for the third time—a truth that any witness watching Kershaw in October understood. Relievers began to enter games earlier and earlier. Instead of developing pitchers to last long in games, organizations taught them to peak out after 4 or 5 or 6 innings. The strategy accelerated the arrival of pitchers in the major leagues, at a period when organizations lacked the tools to prevent arm injuries.

The case of Shane McClanahan was typical of the dangers of the time. He began for the American League against Kershaw in the All-Star Game. He had Tommy John surgery while at the University of

South Florida. Tampa Bay selected him in the first round of the 2018 draft. His fastball averaged nearly 97 mph, although he threw off-speed pitches most of the time. In four professional seasons, he never threw more than 166.1 innings in a year. In seventy-four professional starts, he reached one hundred pitches only twice. The Rays handled him with extreme caution, wary of overexposure and conscious of his value.

And in 2023, McClanahan suffered the same fate as Sandy Alcántara. Both men needed Tommy John surgery to repair their elbows.

Kershaw wasted little time after the Dodgers were eliminated from the 2022 postseason by San Diego. In September, he and Ellen decided to stay in Los Angeles for another season. When he became a free agent, Kershaw conducted his own contract negotiations with Andrew Friedman.

Their connection had improved over time. After Ellis was dealt in 2016, Kershaw kept his distance from Friedman for several months. During a trip to Colorado in early 2017, Friedman asked Kershaw if they could stroll together after a game. Friedman explained his reasoning for trading away Kershaw's close pal. It would have been easier not to make the move, Friedman told Kershaw, but the tiny gain outweighed the risk. "I said that, seeing how competitive he is, I hoped one point that resonated with him was that we are incredibly focused on doing anything and everything we can to win," Friedman told me afterwards.

Friedman admired Kershaw's energy, dedication, and insight into players. He frequently contacted Kershaw before making trade deadline acquisitions. He also praised Kershaw's ease in conducting free-agent talks. "It's been great," Friedman said. "Just direct and honest. "Exactly how you would hope it would go." Friedman benefited from Kershaw's decision. It is considerably easier to haggle with a man who has limited his options. "Like, I'm not going to play for the Phillies," Kershaw explained. "I'm not going to do that." He continued, "It's never going to be like, 'Oh, yeah, let's go see what the Yankees have to offer.'" Kershaw did not want a protracted, nasty holdout, as Derek Jeter did with the Yankees following the 2010 season. The Dodgers declined to force his hand with another qualifying offer. On November 11, six days after the World Series ended, Kershaw agreed to a one-year, $20 million contract in 2023.

Kershaw had just given the Rangers, who had won 68 games, a passing thought. He called Young to inform him that he was returning to Los Angeles before Texas could make a serious offer. (According to people familiar with the issue, the Rangers were considering asking President George W. Bush, who owned the team when Nolan Ryan pitched there, to lobby Kershaw.) Ellen left "the most heartfelt voicemail" for Young's wife, Liz, Young said. Kershaw asked Young to keep him in mind for the future. Young told Kershaw that baseball would not harm their relationship. "I value his friendship, the person he is, and our kids growing up in the same community, all of that, much more than I do anything on the baseball field," Young told me at the time.

"I love the Rangers," Jim Melson told me in December 2022. "I would like to think of him as a Ranger. But it's difficult for me to picture."

Kershaw showed little signs of grumpiness on set. He spoke with the director, the grips, and the wardrobe folks. He rushed through the scenes. He did dozens of takes. He altered his costume multiple times. He trained until the term "Stretch Fit Skechers Slip-Ins" no longer tripped his tongue. There was one line of dialogue—"The stretching is my favorite part"—that struck him as absurd, but he did not disagree. That would simply lengthen his time on stage. After numerous takes pretending to extend an SUV into a limousine, the director declared himself satisfied with the day's work: "That's it for

Clayton Kershaw!"

The crew applauded him in the parking lot outside the ballpark. It was 2:33 p.m. He rushed to get his belongings. He wrote his autograph on a couple baseballs. On his way out of the stadium, a RoughRiders employee stopped him.

"Do you have time for a staff photograph?" Kershaw smiled grimly. "I have to pick up my kids in twenty-one minutes," he informed me. "So I have one minute," he said, posing in the center of the image. He signed another baseball contract. He paused with another employee for a selfie. He hurried to his car. School would end in eighteen minutes. He dreaded being late.

CHAPTER 11
CYCLES OF A CHAMPION

*T*en months later, Clayton Kershaw welcomed me back into his Highland Park home. Cali and Charley were attending school across the street. Cooper drove Chance in a push vehicle through the living room. Later that night, the Texas Rangers would meet the Arizona Diamondbacks in Game 1 of the 2023 World Series in Arlington. Kershaw did not intend to attend. "Definitely not," he replied. "No, I think that would be weird."

There were more important issues for the home. Carpets needed to be cleaned. Kershaw had to choose a Halloween costume; one year he went as the Incredible Hulk, another as Will Ferrell's Jackie Moon, and in numerous others, he skipped trick-or-treating to throw in the World Series. He needed to establish the timeline for his first surgery, which would heal his left shoulder. And he needed to overcome his stoicism and communicate his emotions. He thought his faith hinged on it.

"I'll be honest with you," he informed me. "Faith-wise, the last year has been harder for me." He realized his connection to God had weakened. "You're supposed to feel the presence of the Holy Spirit when you pray," he told me. "And I have a terrible prayer life. I can't pray well. I have difficulty expressing my emotions."

His internal compass could only sustain him for so long. The 2023 season had hurt his physique, tarnished his image, and harmed his pride. At times, he felt lonely, hazy, and unclear about his role in baseball. As Kershaw faced the three-pronged crossroads once more, he was unclear how to proceed. He couldn't articulate his desires, in part because the solutions had earlier seemed so simple. Those close to him, including Ellen and A. J. Ellis challenged him to dig under the surface. It didn't come easily.

"I don't think I've ever made a big decision in my life," he informed me. Consider it. I knew I'd get drafted and wouldn't be able to attend college. I also knew I'd marry Ellen, whom I had a long-term relationship with. That was easy. I spent my entire life playing for the Dodgers. There are no actual decisions there.

"And this offseason, there were about four or five important decisions that I had to make all at once. And it hit me like a tonne of bricks. And it was difficult. You're come at a good time, since I'm much clearer than I was in the previous 10 days."

He had made one decision: he would undergo surgery rather than retire. The operation may be followed by a more surprising choice. When he told me how he imagined the offseason would go, his voice quieted down. He hadn't thrown his final pitch. But he may have delivered his final pitch for the Los Angeles Dodgers.

"Gun to my head, I think I want to play here," Kershaw admitted. "I think I want to leave LA."

Back in March, as we sat outside the Dodgers' clubhouse at Camelback Ranch, it seemed implausible to play for another team.

"I'll tell you what," Kershaw recently told me. "If I was to win another World Series, I think I can't imagine ending it any better than that."

What happened? How did Kershaw transition from picturing a farewell celebration in Los Angeles to planning his departure?

There was no single, irreversible break between Kershaw and the only professional franchise he had ever known. The erosion of their ties occurred gradually. His dissatisfaction with the Dodgers became clear that spring, following a lethargic summer in which Andrew Friedman did not invest to remedy personnel problems. Kershaw had not planned to be present for the majority of spring training. He had planned to pitch for side USA in the World Baseball Classic, which would be beneficial to the American side, which has failed to obtain the participation of its most famous players in the showcase. His participation was cut short when the exhibition's insurance company assessed his injury history and failed to insure him. The restrictions existed to allay teams' concerns about athletes competing in tough competition just days before the regular season began. Without insurance, the Dodgers would be liable for Kershaw's $20 million if he was injured during the tournament.

The Dodgers refused to waive the condition. Kershaw considered buying his own insurance policy but balked at the cost. The event enraged him. He had received calls all winter from Team USA officials urging him to play. He consented to take part, unlike elite American pitchers Max Scherzer, Justin Verlander, Gerrit Cole, Corbin Burnes, and others. Then he was denied permission and forced to endure the rigors of spring training. His two closest Dodgers pals were competing in the event, with Austin Barnes catching for Team Mexico and Trayce Thompson playing outfield for Great Britain. For the majority of the spring, Kershaw believed his closest confidant was massage therapist Possum Nakajima.

The roster turnover had left him without any friends. A. J. Ellis has been absent for years. The same goes for Brett Anderson and Brandon McCarthy, Zack Greinke and Rich Hill, Jamey Wright and Josh Lindblom. Joc Pederson, who frequently drove with Kershaw to Dodger Stadium when it wasn't the fifth day, left after 2020. Mookie Betts and Freddie Freeman replaced Justin Turner and Corey Seager in the Dodgers lineup. Rick Honeycutt has retired. John Pratt accepted a position with the Los Angeles Angels. Tyler Anderson inked a multi-year contract with the Angels. Even Kenley Jansen, the closer who caught Kershaw in the Gulf Coast League, the goofy trash-talker whom Kershaw schooled in backyard basketball in

Midland, Michigan, and the only reliever the Dodgers had ever trusted to replace Kershaw late in games, was pitching elsewhere. "I miss him," Jansen told me. "It's a part of me that I feel has gone."

Kershaw attempted to be pleasant with all of the new faces. The younger pitchers idolized him but couldn't connect with him. Kershaw admired Betts' brilliance and Freeman's dependability, but the two were not close. His relationship with Roberts remained friendly, but distant. Kershaw asked me numerous times while reporting on this book whether I wanted to interview Roberts. He was always concerned about what his manager would say about him. "I have a closer relationship with a lot of other players," Roberts told me, "because that's simply not how he's wired." But our relationship works. It took a long time. When I mentioned that situation as challenging, Roberts concurred. "It is very difficult," he stated. "But he's worth it."

Roberts and Kershaw shared a common purpose. "There's only one reason to keep doing this," Kershaw added. "And that's to win." As he gazed around his clubhouse, he wondered if that ambition was realistic for 2023. Those aspirations were dashed early in camp, when rookie shortstop Gavin Lux sustained a season-ending knee injury. "This is the worst team I've been with," Kershaw stated. Which is difficult to speak aloud. But I believe it is accurate." I questioned if he meant in terms of personality. "Just talent," he explained.

He was mistaken about that. The Dodgers won 100 games and won the National League West for the tenth time in eleven seasons. However, Kershaw found the journey to be far from delightful.

On the evening of March 28, two days before the season began and four days before his first start, Kershaw flew to Dallas. He spent the next morning preparing pancakes with his kids before taking Cali and Charley to school. He spent all afternoon playing with the youngsters. The next morning, he boarded a private jet back to California. "And the flight was delayed," Ellen explained. Her phone flooded with texts from Kershaw, his anxiety mounting as he waited on the tarmac in Phoenix, unable to assert control. "I was like, 'He's having kittens on this plane right now,'" Ellen said.

Kershaw got to Dodger Stadium on time. On April 1, he dismantled the Diamondbacks over six innings. After the game, a mob gathered near Kershaw's locker. Before he could get there, a new comrade stopped him. J. D. Martinez was a five-time All-Star who had never played for the Dodgers before. In the clubhouse earlier that afternoon, he attempted to strike up a discussion with Kershaw. He apologized after the game, explaining that he was unaware of the fifth day. Kershaw waved Martinez away.

"I'm not as crazy as people say I am," he told me.

Ellen and the children traveled to Los Angeles for the game. To commemorate their arrival, Kershaw bought five batches of balloons. "I think I overdid it," he told Ellen. When the children entered the mansion in Studio City, balloons scratched the foyer ceiling. The exhibit remained prominent the following morning, when Kershaw invited me over. The dining room table was overflowing with baby gifts. Ellen was arranging a group baby shower for seven expectant Dodgers couples. Kershaw played catch with Charley for a few minutes outside before leaving for Dodger Stadium. Cooper, the three-year-old, came over as I was speaking with Ellen.

The next two months brought Kershaw success, loneliness, and grief. On April 18, he pitched seven shutout innings against the New York Mets, shouting with rare zeal after striking out with an excellent backdoor slider to preserve a lead and claim his 200th career victory. Tyler Anderson texted him the following morning to congratulate him on his achievement. Kershaw took a bit longer to respond. He'd been lifting in the weight room, locked into the cycle that pointed to another fifth day.

On the surface, he was following the same path. His outcomes were superb. His intensity never wavered. His affable grumpiness persisted. During one game that season, starter Dustin May opened an at-bat with a slider, which pleased pitching coach Mark Prior, who had been urging Kershaw to throw more first-pitch curveballs. "Hey man, we've got every starter to throw first-pitch offspeed," Prior told the crowd. "Not going to happen," Kershaw responded.

Under the surface, he was churning. He was concerned that the front administration would fail to address roster weaknesses by the trade deadline. "We need so much help," Kershaw told me. "I don't think we're going to do it." His left shoulder had begun to throb, filling him with fear. The Dodgers gave him an extra day off between outings; the fifth day became the sixth. When his body refused to comply with the cycle, it became difficult to trust it. He attempted to keep his schedule while flying between Los Angeles and Highland Park, where his mother's health was fast deteriorating. Before the season began, Kershaw paid a visit to Marianne to say farewell, much like he had done with his father in 2013. Throughout the season, however, he returned whenever possible. "She was pretty much asleep," he explained. "It was time. It was time. Alzheimer's, man, is no joke." Marianne died on May 13. Ellen honored her that afternoon in Inglewood, at a ceremony to launch a baseball diamond funded by Kershaw's organization. Marianne, she told the audience of children and parents, had "moved mountains" to help her son's career. "She experienced no greater joy than watching her son grow into the man, the philanthropist, the father, and the ballplayer that he is today," she told the crowd.

Less than a week later, the Dodgers announced a program adjustment for its LGBTQ+ Pride Night on June 16. The Sisters of Perpetual

Indulgence, a group of lesbian and trans people who dressed up as nuns to mock sexual bigotry, were barred from attending. The San Francisco-based group's initial invitation drew criticism from conservative Catholic organizations, including Florida Senator Marco Rubio, who was pressing MLB Commissioner Rob Manfred. When the Dodgers caved to pressure, LGBTQ+ organizations across the country denounced the move. Five days later, the team switched direction and invited the Sisters back to Pride Night.

Kershaw wasn't satisfied with the scenario. He felt the Sisters were mocking his faith. Despite the chaos, he urged the organization to relaunch its Christian Faith and Family Day, which had been postponed since the outbreak. Kershaw announced the event's return via Twitter. He held a players-only meeting to inform his teammates that he planned to speak out against the Sisters, which he did in an interview with the Los Angeles Times. While maintaining that his dissatisfaction "has nothing to do with the LGBTQ community, pride, or anything like that," he criticized the group's methods. "I don't agree with making fun of other people's religions," he told the Times. "It isn't about anything else. I just don't believe that anyone, regardless of their religion, should mock another person's religion."

"I put a lot of thought into it, and talked to a lot of different people," he told me in June. "I suddenly realized that the Dodgers put us in a terrible situation. This is not an LGBT problem. It's just that the group is really nasty. And while I appreciate humor and sarcasm, this goes much beyond that. So I felt the need to say something."

Kershaw was accused of homophobia and bigoted behavior for opposing the Sisters. He considered that his stance was more nuanced. "I'm a sinful person, just like everyone else," he told me. "It is not up to me to condemn or judge others. But there's no way to explain it without people simply canceling you. So you treat everyone the same, and I will do my best to love others as much as I can."

His understanding of his faith led him to speak up. However, it wasn't until months later that he could express the struggle that had possessed him throughout the spring and summer of 2023. He was unsure about the strength of his convictions. His conversation with God had grown fainter. "Sometimes I feel like an imposter when it comes to my faith," he told me in October. "Because baseball has provided a great stage, correct? Talk about anything you desire. And, ultimately, Jesus is what I want to talk about. And I believe that is what God wants me to accomplish with my life: use that platform. But sometimes when you don't feel the Holy Spirit, or I don't feel it, you feel as if you're just putting yourself out there without conviction."

His dilemma was not unusual among adults approaching middle age who were questioning the metaphysical and spiritual. But he was also isolated early in the season, with Ellen and the kids in Texas, while he dealt with the agony in his shoulder and the confusion in his mind. A home stand in early June, following Marianne's death and before his family returned to Los Angeles for the summer, was especially depressing. "Too many hours alone with my thoughts," he explained. "It was just depressing. I mean, I am fine. But at night, it's like, "What am I doing?" Why am I here? I could be home with my children. I am choosing to be away from them right now.'"

What he missed was the life he'd spent his adulthood creating. His partner. His children. His family. "I think when it's your choice to be away from something that you really love, it's harder," he told me.

Two weeks later, I spoke with Chris Young at Yankee Stadium. On his way to the Bronx, Young recalled how he felt entering the ballpark as a player: exhilaration, nervousness, and a surge of competition. "Never to have that again—it's hard," he grumbled. He retired from pitching in 2018. He'd just turned forty-four. His second career had been successful, and the Rangers had emerged as a contender in 2023. But nothing compared to his previous job.

"I would one hundred percent love to be taking that mound tonight, versus doing this job," replied Young. "And I adore what I do. I love it! But I've done my ideal job. That is what Clayton is concerned with. When it's over, it's done."

Very few people write their own endings. For the vast majority, either your body or the game breaks you. Kershaw was one of the few. "My advice for him is to do it as long as he can," Young told me. "You can never get it back."

Young, of course, was biased. He still hoped to sign Kershaw. However, numerous former players mirrored the view. Dan Haren expected to enjoy his newfound independence after retiring in 2015. "It's not easy," Haren explained. "Because everybody believes, 'Oh, I can golf. I can do whatever I want. I can't sit at home watching TV at eleven o'clock in the morning every day. I totally want to shoot myself." After a year, he accepted a position in Arizona's front office. Even then, he continued, "There's been times when I drop my kids at school, go work out, eat lunch, pick them up... It's like, 'Shit, what the hell did I do today?'"'" In the end, Haren admitted, Kershaw would have to deal with the end of his athletic career. It came for them all. "Nothing compares to the life I had from when I was twenty to thirty-five," Haren told me. "It's just a matter of trying to move on, a second phase of life, I guess."

Even Kershaw's oldest pals, who understood the inner agony baseball might cause, agreed. "I can absolutely, totally understand that every fifth day, more than half of a year, you've got this massive anxiety of going through that," Will Skelton told me. "I can imagine wanting to be finished with it. But I imagine you'll never have that feeling again. There is no way to recreate it commercially."

Kershaw sometimes argued that he could live without the feeling. "I have been telling people this for years, and nobody believes it," Kershaw told me in December 2022. "But I don't think I'm competitive unless I'm playing baseball—or Ping-Pong." I began to giggle. "No! That's it!"Kershaw said. "I don't think I'm really competitive. I do not have to win my board games. I don't need to win at cards. I guess I can turn it off." He used the links as an example.

Take golf. Kershaw says he only played four games in the winter following the 2022 season. He made it sound like a little pursuit, a place to pop a beer and have some laughs. Tolleson's wife had, however, given him golf lessons as an anniversary present several years before. When Kershaw learned about this, he hired the instructor. For six weeks, the two maintained the same schedule. They played catch and lifted in the morning, fuelled up for lunch, and then headed to the course. "It's not the instructor's fault, but it was the biggest waste of money that we ever did, because we got so much worse in those six weeks at golf," Tolleson told me afterwards. The tips weakened their inherent athleticism. "It got to the point where we couldn't even hit the ball," Tolleson admitted.

His old teammates questioned if Kershaw was wired for civilian life. "He never skipped a single thing in the nine years that I was there," Justin Turner said. "This is not normal. It's not human." Even away from the diamond, his desire for control manifested in hilarious ways. In his twenties, when he had already married and many of his pals were still single, Kershaw would steal their phones to look into their dating life. Eventually, his friends discovered protection in iPhone passcodes, but Kershaw still cracked a couple. He also used Find My Friends. Meredith was on a business trip when I phoned him in early 2023. "I am sure he'll ask me later this week, 'What were you doing in El Paso?'"" Meredith stated.

Kershaw's final months of 2023 were gloomy, with a disastrous conclusion. On June 27, Kershaw exited a start in Colorado after six scoreless innings and only 79 pitches. His shoulder barked. He was given a cortisone shot to relieve the pain. The injection was limited in its effectiveness. Before the All-Star Game in Seattle, where Kershaw represented the Dodgers for the eleventh time, an MRI revealed that he had damaged his shoulder capsule. A damaged capsule typically necessitated surgery. The rehabilitation could last a year. It was the type of injury that prompted pitchers to consider obtaining a real estate license.

Kershaw buried his face in his hands after hearing the prognosis, Ellen recounted. "Clayton probably felt defeated for ten minutes," Ellen told me. "Then he changed his mindset. And he was like, 'Okay, well, maybe I'll beat the odds on this.'" The end of his career had never felt more imminent. Nonetheless, Kershaw felt he owed his franchise, teammates, and himself nothing short of everything. When he met with team officials to decide how to proceed, Kershaw was "incredibly adamant about pitching," Friedman told me.

The crew never revealed the magnitude of the harm. Neither did Kershaw. His shoulder felt "completely fine," he stated after the All-Star Game. However, he did not return until August 10. At first, he resembled himself, albeit in a shortened, five-inning version. To compensate for his injured shoulder, he adjusted his delivery, resulting in a pinched nerve in his neck that required an epidural. By September, his fastball was sitting around 88 mph, while his slider was approaching 85 mph. The pitch became unexpectedly hittable when the slider's life was shortened.

He didn't seem to enjoy himself. Some pitchers enjoyed coaching younger teammates, and the Dodgers had plenty of them. He worked alongside rookies Bobby Miller, Ryan Pepiot, and Emmet Sheehan. Kershaw did not try to be an additional instructor for them. "This might be, like, harsh, but I really don't have any interest in helping people get better," he told me. "This is certainly selfish, but if it helps Pep and Bobby, I'll go for it. But I don't care." Some pitchers enjoyed the shift from stuff to smarts. Kershaw wasn't one of them. "It's way more fun just to dominate every time," he told me. He had a 2.33

ERA in September, despite only pitching once a week. The sixth day had turned into the seventh day. He procured outs using his reputation rather than his arsenal. He was concerned as the postseason neared, unsure if he could achieve his expectations, even at a reduced capacity. The Dodgers needed him. A series of injuries had destroyed the starting rotation. Julio Urías was on administrative leave after being arrested for felony domestic violence. As Kershaw had feared, the Phillies failed to make an impact at the trade deadline.

In the final month of the season, Kershaw spoke with Roberts, who had already told reporters about Kershaw's physical limitations. The transparency irritated Kershaw, reigniting old grievances with Roberts. The manager argued, as always, that he had Kershaw's best interests at heart. "I was trying to take care of him," Roberts explained. "And he was like, 'Just tell them I stink.'" Kershaw didn't want to confess weakness. "He didn't want that feeling of being a lame doe, where they could smell blood," Roberts told me. The opponents had to believe they were facing Clayton Kershaw, the ten-time All-Star, the finest of his generation, and the last of his kind—not a 35-year-old man with an injured shoulder and an 88-mph fastball.

Late in the season, Kershaw talked with a handful of his younger colleagues about the strain of October baseball. He validated what many people around the Dodgers had suspected about Kershaw as he faced his postseason demons: he was motivated by a dread of failing. "Now," he observed before Game 1 of the National League Division Series against Arizona, "it's just a lot more positive." His optimism couldn't overcome his physical limitations. If the Diamondbacks had any illusions about Kershaw coming into the series, their own hitters crushed them. On the game's second pitch, second baseman Ketel Marte smashed a curveball into center field. The baseball traveled at 115.7 mph, hard enough to clank off rookie center fielder James

Outman's glove. Arizona outran Kershaw after Outman lost the ball and Marte advanced to second base. The Diamondbacks took savage, confident slashes, unconcerned about the broken pitcher's résumé. Kershaw couldn't stop them. He could not produce velocity with his fastball or mislead with his slider. He faced eight hitters. Seven people reached the base. Arizona scored six runs against him, highlighted by a towering homer by rookie catcher Gabriel Moreno. As Moreno's bomb created the left-field fence, Kershaw hung his head and stopped at the waist, resuming his position. Roberts withdrew him with one out in the first inning, and the game was already gone. Kershaw sulked in the dugout as the 11-2 loss proceeded. The outing raised his postseason ERA to 4.49, more than two runs higher than his record-setting regular season ERA.

Following the game, Kershaw approached Ellen. "I'm done," he informed her. He couldn't imagine pitching again. "He was full of emotions," Ellen added. "And, I mean, this is exactly what insanity is: you keep doing it expecting different results and wondering, 'How am I back here?'" Kershaw was overcome by the waste of all the hours he worked and the suffering he underwent in order to be available for October. "You battle all year, you grind," he remarked. "It's been a miserable year trying to be a part of this. And then it happens. And it's like, "That was dumb." Why did I do that?'

On October 31, Kershaw dressed up as Captain America while the kids ran through Highland Park for Halloween. Cali decided to be a sparkly witch. Charley dressed up as George Washington and collected so much candy that he needed a bucket rather than a bag. Cooper was a shark, while Chance was a cow. Two days later, the family headed to Los Angeles. ElAttrache operated on Kershaw's shoulder on November 3. Kershaw slept at ElAttrache's house the night following the procedure. He didn't last very long in a sling. When Charley requested to play catch, Kershaw used his right arm. By November, he was informing pals that he could bring his left arm level with his chest. By December, he believed a return in the summer of 2024 was feasible.

However, as January arrived, Kershaw remained unsigned. After winning the World Series versus Arizona, the Rangers were less aggressive in chasing him than before. Texas officials were concerned about the health of his shoulder while dealing with a cash deficit caused by their exploding television contract. Friedman gave Kershaw space, as he always does. He understood that Kershaw's yearning for a fresh start—which I had also heard him express in those raw moments before the World Series, when the agony and anguish of 2023 were still fresh—was dissipating. Around Christmas, I exchanged emails with a Dodgers staff member who admired Kershaw. "Hopefully," the staffer remarked, "the big guy comes home." The Dodgers were patient with Kershaw while aggressive elsewhere. The team enticed Ohtani with a record-breaking ten-year, $700 million contract, which changed the franchise's financial future. As part of their pitch, Ohtani disclosed at his introductory press conference that Dodgers management admitted they saw the previous ten years of Guggenheim ownership as a failure, despite Kershaw leading the club to three World Series titles and a championship in 2020. That spoke to Ohtani's sensibilities. In an unusual move, Ohtani volunteered to delay $680 million of the money until decades later, effectively serving as a loan that allowed the organization to sign Yamamoto to a twelve-year, $325 million contract. As a bonus, the team traded for Tampa Bay pitcher Tyler Glasnow, who inked a four-year, $110 million contract extension. Glasnow, a skilled but delicate pitcher, threw a career-high 120 innings in 2023, less than Kershaw did with his injured shoulder.

The Dodgers suddenly looked like a superteam again. Only one person went missing. The Dodgers took advantage of the Rangers' lack of enthusiasm. "The recruiting pitch was just trusting me and letting me figure it out on my own," I heard Kershaw say. In January,

Friedman approached Kershaw with a deal tailored to the pitcher's preferences. It was a one-year deal with a $10 million guarantee, a player option for 2025, and a number of incentives: Kershaw would not have to report to spring training until March; he could split his time between Highland Park and Los Angeles while rehabbing; and if he regained his health by the end of the summer, he could return to Los Angeles, where he had spent the previous sixteen years. So in late January, shortly after signing the new contract, he took up a baseball with his surgically repaired left arm and began throwing. It did not feel good. He wouldn't want it any other way. The prospect of another title beckoned. The cycle loomed.

Clayton Kershaw gave his all to his club, teammates, and craft for more than two decades, from childhood to the biggest stage in baseball. He lived in a loop that sustained, tormented, and supplied him with unbelievable wealth. What mattered most to him was the life he had created, the one he led before to Game 1 of the 2023 World Series, a week before his operation. "I don't do anything. "I do everything," he explained. "Every day is unplanned. He unlocked his iPhone and reviewed his daily responsibilities. He was the chosen "ringleader," he stated, for obtaining artificial turf for the elementary school, "so that when it rains, we don't have games canceled." Cali held volleyball games. Charley's basketball season was about to begin, and Kershaw was coaching the squad once again. His immediate plans included lunch with Tolleson, a friend of more than 20 years.

"You look at him and his career, and at face value, here you have a guy who literally has everything," friend and former teammate Josh Lindblom stated. "Everything you could possibly want in a career. But the most essential things to him are the minor details that most people overlook. Having the same pals from high school. Being present for your child's first day at school. These are the things that are most important to him. It's not the Cy Young Awards. It is not the most valuable player. As significant as the World Series is to him, that is not it. It's all the other little details that you might overlook.

On the outside looking in, you wonder, 'Why would he care about that?' Well, he cares because he is Clayton. That is why.

I passed by Clayton Kershaw's house the night before Santa Claus came to Highland Park in the winter of 2022, before he broke his arm and considered leaving Los Angeles. The schoolyard was dark. The streets were vacant. As I rolled past his property, I noticed a pair of tiny children jumping on a trampoline. Outside the safety netting, lighted by Christmas lights, stood their father.

Clayton Kershaw's career will eventually come to an end. His life won't. He will carry on, as a husband, parent, and man. He'll have to give it his best.

The contents of this book may not be copied, reproduced or transmitted without the express written permission of the author or publisher. Under no circumstances will the publisher or author be responsible or liable for any damages, compensation or monetary loss arising from the information contained in this book, whether directly or indirectly. .

Disclaimer Notice:

Although the author and publisher have made every effort to ensure the accuracy and completeness of the content, they do not, however, make any representations or warranties as to the accuracy, completeness, or reliability of the content. , suitability or availability of the information, products, services or related graphics contained in the book for any purpose. Readers are solely responsible for their use of the information contained in this book

Every effort has been made to make this book possible. If any omission or error has occurred unintentionally, the author and publisher will be happy to acknowledge it in upcoming versions.

Printed in Dunstable, United Kingdom